CHEMISTRY

CHEMISTRY

The People Behind the Science

KATHERINE CULLEN, PH.D.

CHELSEA HOUSE
PUBLISHERS
An imprint of Infobase Publishing

Chemistry: The People Behind the Science

Chelsea House
An imprint of Infobase Publishing
132 West 31st Street
New York NY 10001

Library of Congress Cataloging-in-Publication Data

Cullen, Katherine E.
   Chemistry: the people behind the science/Katherine Cullen.
     p. cm. — (Pioneers in science)
   Includes bibliographical references and index.
   ISBN 0-8160-5462-2 (acid-free paper)
   1. Chemists—Biography—Popular works. 2. Women chemists—Biography—Popular works. 3. Chemistry—History—Popular works. 4. Discoveries in science—Popular works. I. Title. II. Series
     QD21.C85 2005
     540'.92'2—dc22   2005022276

Chelsea House books are available at special discounts when purchased in bulk quantities for businesses, associations, institutions, or sales promotions. Please call our Special Sales Department in New York at (212) 967-8800 or (800) 322-8755.

You can find Chelsea House on the World Wide Web at
http://www.chelseahouse.com

Text design by Mary Susan Ryan-Flynn
Cover design by Cathy Rincon
Illustrations by Bobbi McCutcheon

Printed in the United States of America

MP FOF 10 9 8 7 6 5 4 3 2 1

This book is printed on acid-free paper.

*I dedicate this book to
all future pioneers in science.*

&

CONTENTS

CHAPTER 6

Emil Hermann Fischer (1852–1919): Synthesis of Purines and Sugars and the Mechanism of Enzyme Action 77

CHAPTER 7

Gerty Cori (1896–1957): Sugar Metabolism and Glycogen Storage Disorders 89

PREFACE

Being first in line earns a devoted fan the best seat in the stadium. The first runner to break the ribbon spanning the finish line receives a gold medal. The firstborn child inherits the royal throne. Certain advantages or privileges often accompany being the first, but sometimes the price paid is considerable. Neil Armstrong, the first man to walk on the Moon, began flying lessons at age 16, toiled at numerous jobs to pay tuition, studied diligently to earn his bachelor's degree in aerospace engineering, flew 78 combat missions in Korea as a brave navy pilot, worked as a civilian test pilot for seven years, then as an astronaut for NASA for another seven years, and made several dangerous trips into space before the historic *Apollo 11* mission. He endured rigorous physical and mental preparation, underwent years of training, and risked his life to courageously step foot where no man had ever walked before. Armstrong was a pioneer of space exploration; he opened up the way for others to follow. Not all pioneering activities may be as perilous as space exploration. But like the ardent fan, a pioneer in science must be dedicated; like the competitive runner, she must be committed; and like being born to royalty, sometimes providence plays a role.

Science encompasses all knowledge based on general truths or observed facts. More narrowly defined, science refers to a branch of knowledge that specifically deals with the natural world and its laws. Philosophically described, science is an endeavor, a search for truth, a way of knowing, or a means of discovering. Scientists gain information through employing a procedure called the scientific method. The scientific method requires one to state the problem and formulate a testable hypothesis or educated guess to describe a phenomenon or explain an observation, test the hypothesis experimentally or by collecting data from observations, and draw conclusions from the results. Data can eliminate a hypothesis, but never confirm it with absolute certainty; scientists may accept a hypothesis as true when sufficient supporting evidence has been obtained. The process sounds entirely straightforward, but sometimes advancements in science do not follow such a logical approach. Because humans make the observations, generate the hypothesis, carry out the experiments, and draw the conclusions, students of science must recognize the personal dimension of science.

Pioneers in Science is a set of volumes that profile the people behind the science, individuals who initiated new lines of thought or research. They risked possible failure and often faced opposition but persisted to pave new pathways of scientific exploration. Their backgrounds vary tremendously; some never graduated from secondary school, while others earned multiple advanced degrees. Familial affluence allowed some to pursue research unhindered by financial concerns, but others were so poor they suffered from malnutrition or became homeless. Personalities ranged from exuberant to somber and gentle to stubborn, but they all sacrificed, giving their time, insight, and commitment because they believed in the pursuit of knowledge. The desire to understand kept them going when they faced difficulties, and their contributions moved science forward.

The set consists of eight separate volumes: *Biology; Chemistry; Earth Science; Marine Science; Physics; Science, Technology, and Society; Space and Astronomy;* and *Weather and Climate.* Each book contains 10 biographical sketches of pioneering individuals in a subject, including information about their childhood, how they entered into their scientific careers, their research, and enough background science information for the reader to appreciate their discoveries and contributions. Though all the profiled individuals are certainly distinguished, their inclusion is not intended to imply that they are the greatest scientists of all time. Rather, the profiled individuals were selected to reflect a variety of subdisciplines in each field, different histories, alternative approaches to science, and diverse characters.

Each chapter includes a chronology and a list of specific references about the individual and his work. Each book also includes an introduction to the field of science to which its pioneers contributed, line illustrations, photographs, a glossary of scientific terms related to the research described in the text, and a listing of further resources for information about the general subject matter.

The goal of this set is to provide, at an appropriate level, factual information about pioneering scientists. The authors hope that readers will be inspired to achieve greatness themselves, to feel connected to the people behind science, and to believe that they may have a positive and enduring impact on society.

ACKNOWLEDGMENTS

I would like to thank Frank K. Darmstadt, Executive Editor of science and mathematics at Infobase Publishing, for his skillful guidance and extreme patience, and to Melissa Cullen-DuPont, for having all the answers. Appreciation is also extended to illustrator Bobbi McCutcheon for her dedicated professionalism and to Ann E. Hicks for her constructive suggestions. The reference librarians and support staff of the main branch of the Medina County District Library, located in Medina, Ohio, deserve acknowledgment for their assistance in obtaining interlibrary loans, acquiring numerous special requests, and handling the hundreds of materials and resources the author borrowed during the writing of this set. Gratitude is also expressed to Pam Shirk, former media specialist at A. I. Root Middle School in Medina, Ohio, for sharing her expertise. Many people and organizations generously gave permission to use their photographs. Their names are acknowledged underneath the donated images. Thank you all.

INTRODUCTION

A limited number of chemical elements make up all matter in the entire universe. The wood of a chair, the salty water filling the ocean basins, a warm-blooded human being, and the hot gaseous mixture of a star that is light-years away can all be defined ultimately by the atoms from which they are made—atoms are the building blocks of all matter. As early as 600 B.C.E., Greek philosophers contemplated the composition of the universe. They speculated that all matter was composed of a single element, such as water or air, but in different densities. Around 450 B.C.E., Empedocles proposed that everything was made of four basic elements in different proportions: air, earth, fire, and water. A century later, Aristotle suggested adding a fifth element, ether, as a ubiquitous substance that filled otherwise unoccupied space. These ideas dominated embryonic *chemistry* notions for a millennium, when the pseudoscience of alchemy became popular in the eighth century. Alchemists were interested in discovering a means to transform common base metals into precious metals such as gold and in finding an elixir capable of curing any ailment and prolonging human life. Though they did not achieve these unfeasible goals, alchemical endeavors did reveal much about the chemical nature of substances and common chemical reactions, eventually progressing into premodern chemistry.

Modern chemistry is the scientific study of the composition and properties of matter, anything with mass that occupies volume. Because chemical principles are fundamental to understanding other scientific subjects, such as biology, physics, and geology, careers in the health sciences, physical sciences, and the Earth sciences all require atom in terms of its weight and to provide evidence for its existence. By the mid-19th century, the list of known elements had expanded into a chaotic chemical conglomeration, until the Siberian chemist Dmitry Mendeleyev discovered a logical means for arranging them, a periodic dependence upon atomic weight, from which he developed the first periodic table of the elements, a keystone of chemistry.

In the early 20th century, the American chemist Irving Langmuir made numerous advancements in the field of surface chemistry that permeated everyday life, including improvements to the lightbulb and techniques for the manufacture of eyeglass lenses. The German chemist Emil Hermann Fischer emphasized the importance of the orientation of atoms in addition to their position within a molecule, a concept crucial in organic chemistry, and helped pioneer the field of biochemistry through his research on sugars and proteins. Gerty Cori advanced the budding field of biochemistry by elucidating the intermediates of the metabolic pathways for sugar metabolism and then went further to link specific enzyme deficiencies to inherited metabolic disorders. Though organic chemists used to believe that organic compounds could only be obtained from living organisms, masters of synthesis such as American Percy Julian developed mechanisms for the manufacture of many chemicals on which modern society depends, such as medicines and insecticides. Linus Pauling was a brilliant scholar who made numerous contributions to chemistry, but his most famous achievement was the explanation of the nature of chemical bonding. In a career that spanned seven decades, structural chemist Dorothy Hodgkin pushed the limits of X-ray crystallography to reveal the structures of molecules that many thought were too complicated. Though set apart by their time periods, their different subdisciplines, and the practical applications of their research, all of the aforementioned chemists are surely pioneers in science.

Joseph Priestley

(1733–1804)

Joseph Priestley is credited with discovering oxygen. *(Library of Congress, Prints and Photographs Division [LC-USZ62-102551])*

The Discovery of Oxygen

Take a deep breath. There is nothing like inhaling fresh, clean air, especially in the countryside. Why is that—the *oxygen?* The environment simply could be more psychologically relaxing than the air is physically healing, yet oxygen does have rejuvenating effects on the body. During the late 1990s, so-called oxygen bars crept into pop culture as an expensive trend, with customers purchasing oxygen that they inhaled through a plastic tube inserted into their nostrils. Users claimed they felt less stressed and had more energy afterward.

More than 200 years ago, one man cautioned that if a healthy person should regularly breathe pure oxygen he might live out his life too quickly. This man was Joseph Priestley. Not only did he discover oxygen, but he also invented carbonated beverages, delineated the process of *photosynthesis*, invented apparatuses that improved the efficiency of gas collection before the word *gas* even existed, and discovered ten new gases himself. This tenacious researcher was trained as a minister but felt that spending time on matters defined as religious was only one way to worship God. Studying natural philosophy (the natural sciences including physics, chemistry, and biology) was another. Priestley felt that understanding the mysteries of natural phenomena was in itself a way to honor God and that it proved his wonder and omnipotence. So was Priestley a theologian or scientist? Limiting the choices to these two professions is not sufficient. He also advanced the fields of political science, language and grammar, philosophy, history, and many more.

Strict Calvinist Upbringing

Joseph Priestley was the oldest of six children born to Jonas Priestley and his first wife, Mary Swift, on March 13, 1733. They lived in Fieldhead, England, near Yorkshire, where the father was a cloth merchant. As the family grew, Joseph was sent to live temporarily with his maternal grandparents. His mother died during the birth of her sixth child in as many years, and at age nine Joseph was sent to live with his aunt, Sarah Priestley Keighley, until adulthood.

The Keighley household was strict Calvinist, meaning they believed in salvation by God's grace alone, God's omnipotence, predestination, and original sin, among other things. Joseph was exposed to several religious viewpoints, as dissenting ministers were often invited to their home. *Dissenters* were people who did not accept the doctrines of the Church of England. While simply having nonconformist beliefs was not illegal, there were specific laws that limited the privileges of those who did not subscribe to the national religion.

By the time he was a teenager, it was obvious that Joseph was a prodigy. He had already mastered several languages and was tutored privately in algebra, geometry, and Newtonian mechanics, but he felt called to the ministry. Ironically, as a young adult he was denied admission into the church in which he was raised because he could not accept the doctrine of original sin. He did not believe that all humanity was inherently evil and deserved to suffer. Since he was not a communicant of the Church of England, he was not permitted admission at the highly regarded Oxford or Cambridge Universities. So at age 19, he became the first student to enroll in the dissenting academy at Daventry. While there, he enjoyed the inquiry-based learning atmosphere and spent lots of time formulating his thoughts concerning different religious doctrines.

A Popular Teacher

He left the academy in 1755 and took a position as an assistant minister at Needham Market in Suffolk. As Priestley's personal religious beliefs matured, his congregation and senior minister became uncomfortable with his viewpoints, in particular, his denial of the Trinity, or the union of the Father, the Son, and the Holy Ghost. When he had fulfilled the obligations of his term, he anxiously accepted a position as a minister at Nantwich, in Cheshire. To supplement his income there, he opened a successful school for the girls and boys in his congregation. His own interests in natural philosophy increased, and he purchased an air pump and an electrical machine that his students used for experiments.

His reputation as a teacher grew, and in 1761, Priestley was invited to join the faculty at the dissenting academy at Warrington, in the county of Lancashire. While at Warrington, he became ordained and enjoyed the company of fellow Arian faculty. (Arians believe that Jesus was above other created beings but not divine like God.) He began to write and publish successful texts on language, grammar, and education and conducted electrical experiments. In 1764, he was awarded a doctor of law degree from the University of Edinburgh for his studies on education. Priestley remained at Warrington for six years, until the income was no longer enough to support his growing family. He had married Mary Wilkinson, the sister of one of his former students, on June 23, 1762, and they already had one daughter.

While traveling to London in 1766, Priestley met Benjamin Franklin, an American statesman who was representing the colonies in discussions with the British government. Franklin was a respected scientist who had made the famous discovery that lightning was an electrical phenomenon. Priestley took advantage of this opportunity to discuss his electrical experiments with Franklin. Franklin encouraged Priestley to write his *History and Present State of Electricity, with Original Experiments*, a text that gave an up-to-date accounting of all related research. Franklin even assisted Priestley in obtaining reference material. One new observation from Priestley's own experiments was that *carbon*, a nonmetal, could conduct electricity. He reported his deduction that the electrical attraction between bodies had an inverse-square relationship to the distance between them. He also recorded the first description of an oscillatory discharge, the same principle used in wireless telegraphy by the Italian inventor Guglielmo Marconi. Even before the book, which was published in 1767, reached the shops, news of Priestley's experiments had spread among other English scientists. In 1766, he was elected a fellow of the Royal Society on the basis of his electrical work, quite an honor for someone with no formal training in science.

The position at Warrington did not offer the Priestley family the financial security they desired, and Joseph missed the ministry. By this time, Priestley had come to accept all the doctrines of an extreme Unitarian. Unitarianism denies the trinity, believing that God is one, not three. Unitarians generally are tolerant of different religious beliefs, believing that a person's conscience may act as the authority on religious matters and that the Bible is fallible. In 1767, he moved his family to Leeds and took over the Presbyterian parish at Mill-Hill Chapel.

The Invention of Carbonated Beverages

A minister at heart but also fully a scientist, Priestley could not ignore the unusual odor that came from the brewery next door to their new home. He became particularly interested in the air over the fermentation vats and obtained permission from the brewery owner to explore this phenomenon. This initiated his experiments in *pneumatic chemistry*, the chemistry of airs. (The term *gas* had not yet been coined.)

Priestley climbed to the top of the large fermenting vats and made observations. He saw a cloud hanging over the vats. When he waved at it, the cloud sank to the ground, suggesting that whatever its composition, it was heavier than ordinary air. He also noticed that when he put a candle to it, the air would extinguish the flame. Priestley wanted to see if this air dissolved in water. He put a pan of water very close to one of the vats and let some of the air fall into it. Then he mixed it up and let more fall in until he was sure no more of the heavy air could dissolve in the water. The gas was mostly soluble, but some tiny bubbles floated to the top, resembling the expensive seltzer water from natural springs. Dying of curiosity, he sipped some, and it even tasted like seltzer water. His excitement grew.

After days of going back and forth between the brewery and his home trying to collect the air over the vats in bottles to play with it at home in his wife's kitchen, he thought perhaps he could produce this special air on his own. He recalled reading that a Scottish chemist named Joseph Black made what was called "fixed air" by heating limestone. The fixed air, which today is called *carbon dioxide*, also had the characteristic of extinguishing flames. Priestley tried Black's method, but after some experimenting he had better luck heating chalk with water and adding "marine acid" (today called hydrochloric acid).

To collect the carbon dioxide, he filled a tub with water, inverted a bottle filled with water with the mouth covered, and then removed the cover after setting the inverted bottle in the tub. He connected a tube running from the apparatus in which he mixed chemicals or heated substances to the opening of the inverted bottle. If a gas was formed and it was lighter than water, it would rise up inside the inverted bottle and displace some of the water down out of the mouth. The amount of gas produced was related to the amount of water displaced. This apparatus is called a *pneumatic trough*.

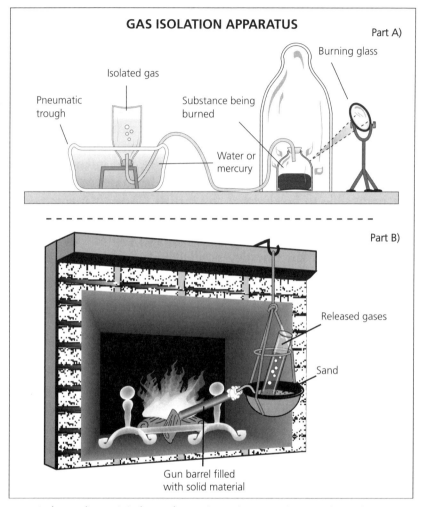

GAS ISOLATION APPARATUS

Part A)

Burning glass

Isolated gas

Pneumatic trough

Substance being burned

Water or mercury

Part B)

Released gases

Sand

Gun barrel filled with solid material

Liquids (part A) or solids (part B) were heated using a burning lens. The gases were collected using a pneumatic trough. Sometimes solids were heated over a fire in a gun barrel.

"Observations on Different Kinds of Air." Other discoveries were published in his six-volume series titled *Experiments and Observations on Different Kinds of Air and Other Branches of Natural Philosophy*, published during the period 1774–86. Because of his advancements in the field of pneumatic chemistry, Priestley was elected to the French Academy of Sciences.

The Discovery of Oxygen

Once again, the financial strain of supporting his family lured Priestley into new employment. In 1773, William Fitzmaurice Petty, the second earl of Shelburne, hired him as his librarian, literary companion, and supervisor of his sons' education. Lord Shelburne promised him not only a generous salary but also a well-equipped laboratory and an extra stipend to purchase chemicals and supplies for experiments. Taking this position also meant moving his family to Calne, in Wiltshire. Priestley spent the summers with his family and the winters with Lord Shelburne in London. His years with Shelburne, from 1773 to 1780, were by far his most productive in the advancement of chemistry. Most of the work presented in his *Airs* series was performed during these years.

In August of 1774, for no obvious reason, Priestley burned mercurius calcinatus (red mercuric oxide) using a large magnifying lens. He collected the resultant gas using his usual method of passing it through mercury into an inverted bottle. Shiny globules of elemental mercury were left behind. He collected three bottles full of the released gas. Because he had a lit candle nearby, he held it to the gas in one bottle, and the flame burned brighter. He took a glowing ember of wood and held it to the second bottle, and it immediately burst into flames. Even more remarkably, a mouse could live trapped in a bottle with this air longer than with ordinary air.

At the time, scientists widely accepted the phlogiston theory to explain how materials burned. They believed that a substance called phlogiston was responsible for allowing things to burn. If a substance had a lot of phlogiston, it burned easily; if a substance had little phlogiston, then it was more resistant to burning. When all the phlogiston had left a substance, burning would cease. The fact that a candle flame would be extinguished if kept under a jar was explained by the air becoming saturated with phlogiston, thus it could absorb no more and the flame would die. Because the new air that Priestley had extracted from mercurius calcinatus allowed the candle and the ember to burn more brightly, he reasoned that the air produced had little to no phlogiston present in it. Because of this, it was able to suck the phlogiston out of the candle and the wood much more readily. He called this special type of air "dephlogisticated."

Priestley had discovered oxygen. He inhaled some himself and found that it made him feel light and easy. He predicted that breathing this new air would be a good medical treatment for people with respiratory problems, yet he worried that if it were used by healthy persons it may cause one "to live out too fast." He wrote up his results the next year and sent them to the Royal Society in March of 1775.

A Challenge to Phlogiston Theory

During the fall of 1774, Priestley accompanied Lord Shelburne to Europe. One night they dined with other famous scientists including the French chemist Antoine Lavoisier, who was much younger than Priestley but already very respected in the field. He asked Priestley about his current experiments, and Priestley openly shared his exciting discovery of dephlogisticated air. The other scientists were impressed and peppered him with questions, but Lavoisier just listened silently. Unbeknownst to Priestley, Lavoisier was already trying to incorporate this new knowledge into a set of experiments he would perform over the next few months. Lavoisier later repeated Priestley's experiments and presented his own results to the French Academy of Sciences in April of 1775 without giving any credit to Priestley for his intellectual contribution. Lavoisier called the dephlogisticated air "oxygen," from the Greek word *oxys*, which means "sharp" (like an acid), and *gen*, which means "to be born." He also showed that ordinary air is made up of approximately 20 percent oxygen. He went even further by using this information to blast the entire phlogiston theory.

Lavoisier challenged, "If phlogiston is released when something is burned, then why does the weight increase after burning?" He had carefully measured the weight of several materials before and after burning and found this always to be the case. Lavoisier correctly hypothesized that burning, or combustion, resulted from the combination of a substance with oxygen. Candle flames were extinguished in enclosed spaces due to the oxygen being used up. Mice died after a while under a jar for the same reason. Priestley could not accept this—he believed that phlogiston had a quality called levity, a sort of negative weight. He thought the explanation of phlogiston saturation was sufficient to explain why candle flames burned out after a period of time. Another problem with the phlogiston theory was that phlogiston had never been isolated. To this, Priestley responded that neither gravity nor electricity nor magnetism had been isolated and that phlogiston resembled a power more than a substance.

Priestley did not make a fuss after Lavoisier tried to steal the rights to the discovery of dephlogisticated air, or oxygen. He believed that the importance was the discovery itself and that benefits could be derived no matter who got credit for it. Priestley searched for truth, not fame.

Studies on Photosynthesis

After identifying so many different airs, Priestley began to wonder more about how ordinary air was purified. In Leeds, he learned that green plants were capable of cleaning bad air and replacing it with pure air. He decided to pursue this by filling several bottles with

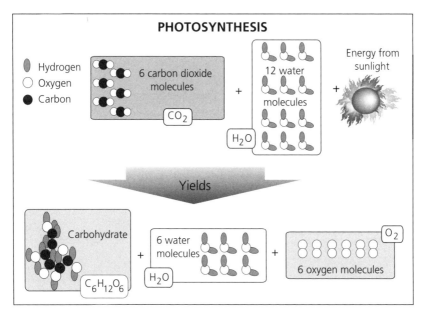

In the process of photosynthesis, energy from light is harnessed and stored in chemical compounds called carbohydrates. Carbon dioxide is consumed and oxygen is released.

How Plants Make Food

Almost all living organisms eventually satisfy their energy needs through a process called photosynthesis, the conversion of light energy into chemical energy that is stored in organic *compounds*. Even carnivores, or meat-eaters, ultimately depend on organisms that directly obtain their energy from organisms that undergo photosynthesis. The chloroplast is the structure capable of undergoing photosynthesis in plants and some protists. Chloroplasts are specialized membrane-bound organelles that contain the pigment chlorophyll, which absorbs the red and blue light of the visible spectrum. Because green light is reflected, most photosynthetic organisms are the color green or at least have green parts. One square millimeter of a leaf contains approximately 500,000 chloroplasts.

water and inverting them over bowls containing water. Some of the bottles had green pond scum (probably algae) in the water, and some did not. All of them were placed outside in the sunlight. By the end of the day, the water had been displaced in the bottles over the scummy water but not in the bottles over the plain water. A gas had been produced in the presence of the pond scum. When he placed a glowing ember in the gas and it burst into flames, he realized that the green plants (or algae) had produced oxygen. Priestley wondered if the fact that green plants required sunlight to survive was related to their oxygen-producing capability. He repeated the experiment, but this time he put some of the bottles in the dark. No oxygen was produced, demonstrating that light was required. This well-researched process is termed *photosynthesis*.

Controversial Works

The initial years with Shelburne were enjoyable and productive. Priestley and Shelburne had much in common; for example, they

When energy in the form of light is absorbed by chlorophyll, *electrons* of the chlorophyll *molecules* jump to higher energy levels and begin a cascade of falling step by step to sequentially lower energy levels in a chain of molecules. Water molecules that supply the electrons from their hydrogen *atoms* are split, and the oxygen is released as a by-product. The hydrogen atoms donate electrons to the chlorophyll molecules, and the remaining *protons* are used to create a proton gradient. The energy harvested from the sunlight, now in the form of a chemical and electrical gradient, drives the synthesis of adenosine triphosphate (ATP), a form of chemical energy readily useable by the cell, and nicotinamide adenine dinucleotide phosphate (NADPH), an electron carrier molecule. Both the ATP and the NADPH then are used to reduce carbon, supplied in the form of carbon dioxide (CO_2), in order to synthesize *carbohydrates*, or *sugars*. In summary, photosynthetic organisms use sunlight, CO_2, and water to produce sugars, releasing oxygen in the process.

both sympathized with the American colonists for the troubles they were having with the British Parliament. Lord Shelburne was a member of the cabinet, however, and supported the colonies remaining under British rule, whereas Priestley supported their freedom and independence. At some point Priestley's radical opinions that Shelburne previously appreciated became too controversial. In addition, the publishing of Priestley's recent pamphlet, entitled *The Disinquisitions on Matter and Spirit,* caused quite a stir. In it, Priestley basically denied the existence of souls without a physical body. The relationship between Priestley and Lord Shelburne slowly cooled. In 1780, Lord Shelburne politely offered him a position in Ireland, but Priestley declined.

The Priestley family had grown to a total of four children, and they wanted to stay in England. Priestley accepted a position as minister at the New Meetinghouse in Birmingham, Warwickshire. By original agreement, despite their parting, Priestley continued to receive an annuity from Lord Shelburne. While at Warwickshire, Priestley joined the Lunar Society, a group of men who met on nights when the moon was full. Other members included James Watt (of steam engine fame), Josiah Wedgwood, John Smeaton, Matthew Boulton, and Erasmus Darwin in addition to others of high reputation. They freely discussed religious, scientific, and political matters, and Priestley thrived on the intellectual stimulation.

In January of 1781, Priestley decided to carry out some experiments attempting to convert air to water and vice versa. He put a piece of minium, red lead (Pb_3O_4), into a container filled with inflammable air over water. When he focused the rays from a burning lens on it, the minium turned black and then into pure lead while the air volume decreased and the water level ascended in the receiver. Was the air being absorbed by the water? The next day, he combined inflammable air with common air and sent an electrical spark through it. A crackle resulted, and moisture appeared on the inside of the container. Did the air turn into water? Priestley wrote to the discoverer of inflammable air, English chemist Henry Cavendish, who examined this phenomenon further. Thanks to Priestley's observation and willingness to share scientific knowledge, Cavendish was able to determine the composition of water to be two parts hydrogen and one part oxygen, H_2O.

In 1782, Priestley published yet another controversial work, a two-volume project called *History of the Corruptions of Christianity*. This work vehemently attacked many of the beliefs of the Church of England. Then he wrote *History of Early Christian Opinions Regarding Jesus Christ* (1786), declaring that Jesus was just a man. He also published annual pamphlets defending the doctrines of Unitarianism. Political and religious tensions continued to grow.

On the night of the second anniversary of the storming of Bastille (a key event of the French Revolution), July 14, 1791, several friends and Priestley planned to meet at a local inn for dinner. For some reason, Priestley ended up staying home and playing backgammon with his wife that evening. Suddenly they heard noises outside. A neighbor was rushing to tell them that the inn had been stormed by a "Church-and-King" mob. He feared that Priestley was the real target, so Priestley's family immediately fled to a friend's house, and then Joseph snuck out of town to London.

By the end of that night, the mob had destroyed his house, his laboratory, and his church.

The Priestleys were forced to move again. Joseph found a job preaching at Gravel Pit Meeting in Hackney, but their life was not comfortable. Priestley had defended the rights of Americans to break away from Britain, he sympathized with the French revolutionaries, and he had consistently chipped away at the heart of the nation's prescribed religion. His own religious views were unpopular, and he had preached them too loudly for too long. Priestley was shunned by his former Royal Society colleagues, and he and his wife no longer felt welcome in their motherland. They began to think they might be happier in the United States, where their three sons had moved a few years earlier.

Immigration to America

Joseph and Mary Priestley set sail for America in April of 1794. Though practically chased out of England, the United States warmly greeted Priestley. They stayed in New York for a few weeks and then moved on to Philadelphia. Priestley had become a member of the American Philosophical Society (founded by Ben Franklin) and wanted to visit some of the members there, though his old friend and confidante, Ben Franklin, had died in 1790. The Priestleys moved in with their son Joseph until their own house was complete. A laboratory was set up after the surprise arrival of several pieces of equipment sent from Josiah Wedgwood and others from England. One and one-half years after their arrival, their youngest son, Henry, died of pneumonia. Nine months later, Mary died.

Though most of his time was spent puttering in his lab, writing religious texts, and corresponding with colleagues including Thomas Jefferson, Benjamin Rush, and John Adams, Priestley continued to keep up with new developments in chemistry. He hoped to determine the amount of phlogiston in various metals. In 1799 he discovered yet another new gas, carbon monoxide, by heating coal in a small amount of air. Though poisonous, this gas has many industrial uses. He continued to passionately defend the phlogiston theory despite the fact that it had been demolished, ironically, as a

FURTHER READING

Garraty, John A., and Mark C. Carnes, eds. *American National Biography*. Vol. 17. New York: Oxford University Press, 1999. Brief account of the lives and works of famous Americans in encyclopedia format.

Gillispie, Charles C., ed. *Dictionary of Scientific Biography*. Vol. 11. New York: Scribner, 1970–76. Good source for facts concerning personal background and scientific accomplishments but assumes basic knowledge of science.

Horvitz, Leslie Alan. *Eureka! Scientific Breakthroughs that Changed the World*. New York: John Wiley, 2002. Explores the events and thought processes that led 12 great minds to their eureka moments.

"Joseph Priestley." Chemical Heritage Foundation, 2000. Available online. URL: http://www.chemheritage.org/EducationalServices/ chemach/fore/jp.html. Accessed February 1, 2005. Part of the chemical achievers biographical profile series aimed at middle and high school students.

Marcus, Rebecca B. *Joseph Priestley: Pioneer Chemist*. New York: Franklin Watts, Inc., 1961. An older resource, but gives detailed descriptions of the discovery of each new gas. Easy reading.

Saari, Peggy, and Stephen Allison, eds. *The Lives and Works of 150 Scientists*. Vol. 3. Detroit, Mich.: U*X*L, 1996. Alphabetically arranged introductions to the contributions of scientists from a variety of fields. Intended for middle school students.

Schofield, Robert E. *The Enlightenment of Joseph Priestley: A Study of His Life and Work from 1733 to 1773*. University Park, Pa.: Pennsylvania State University Press, 1997. Discussion of scientific, theological, political, and other activities during Priestley's first 40 years. Difficult reading.

water could be changed into the element of earth, which included any solid substance. He set up an experiment where he carefully washed, dried, and weighed a glass flask. Then he added a precisely measured sample of highly pure water, sealed the vessel, and heated it to barely boiling for 101 days. As expected, sediment eventually appeared in the flask. Had water been converted into earth? He weighed the vessel with its contents and found the total weight was the same as before heating. He then separated the water from the newly formed sediment and the flask and carefully weighed each once again. The water weighed the same as before heating, but the glass vessel had decreased in weight by exactly the same amount as the weight of the particulate residue. This indicated that water was not being converted to earth, but that some substance had been dissolved from the vessel by prolonged heating. These results, read to the academy in 1770, demonstrated the importance of careful measurement during experimentation.

The Oxygen Theory of Combustion

The next scientific problem Lavoisier worked on was combustion, or burning. In the early 1770s, Lavoisier used large magnifying lenses to burn diamond that several scientists had jointly purchased. He found that even though in the presence of fresh air the solid diamond could be completely burned into what we today refer to as carbon dioxide gas, the total weight remained unchanged. In conjunction with his previous experiments that led him to conclude that water did not transmutate into earth, this experiment led him to formulate the law of conservation of mass. This law states that mass can neither be created nor destroyed during a *chemical reaction.* Gases previously had not been considered as reactants or products in chemical processes, but Lavoisier emphasized the importance of recognizing the gaseous state.

The German chemists Johann Becher and Georg Stahl had proposed the phlogiston theory at the end of the 17th century as an attempt to explain how materials burned. According to this theory, fire could act as an element called phlogiston. Substances that contained a lot of this element, such as oil or charcoal, would burn easily. During burning, phlogiston was released into the air. Materials that contained no phlogiston could not burn. One major flaw with this widely accepted theory was that after metals were burned, their *calces* (the burned products) weighed more than the original metals had weighed prior to burning. If during the process of burning the metals were losing phlogiston, then why did they weigh more instead of less than their original weight? Phlogiston supporters responded that phlogiston had negative weight, or buoyancy. This annoyed Lavoisier, who thought a much more logical explanation was that something had been added to the metals. He felt that supporters of the phlogiston theory subjectively rearranged their experiments in an attempt to prove what they already believed rather than objectively gathering facts to form a theory.

In 1772, Lavoisier started burning different metals, as had others before him. He always meticulously weighed the metals before and after burning. As expected, he found that calces from sulfur, phosphorus, tin, and lead weighed more than the original metals. When he burned these substances in a sealed flask, however, he found that the enclosed air decreased in weight by the same amount that the metals increased in weight. When he opened the container, air rushed in. When he reweighed the flask, the increase in weight equaled the increased weight of the metal calx, suggesting the air that rushed in was replacing air that was absorbed by the metals during burning. He next performed the experiment in reverse by heating the metal calces in the presence of charcoal in a closed container, and he found that lots of air was given off. Afterward the metals weighed less than their calces had originally. From these experiments he proposed that during combustion the metals absorbed some component from the air. He wondered what this could be. Lavoisier presented these results to the Academy in 1773 and published them in his first book, *Opuscules physiques et chimiques* (Essays physical and chemical), in 1774.

In 1774, the Lavoisiers gave a dinner party and invited Joseph Priestley, an English chemist who was visiting Paris. During dinner conversation, Lavoisier learned that Priestley had obtained a different type of air, named dephlogisticated air, by heating mercury calx (now called mercuric oxide) in a closed vessel and collecting the gas released. This air caused candle flames to burn brightly and allowed animals to live in closed containers longer than usual.

Lavoisier had an epiphany. He believed Priestley's dephlogisticated air was involved in combustion. Mercury was a unique metal. Scientists had learned it could be converted from its calx back into its metallic form by heating in the absence of charcoal. Lavoisier repeated his and Priestley's earlier experiments under extremely controlled conditions. When he heated mercury in the presence of common air, after time, no more mercury calx formed, although plenty of mercury remained. Lavoisier guessed that whatever was removed from the air during burning was used up. He determined that one-fifth of the volume of the air had been expended. Only part of the air was involved in the formation of mercury calx. This vital component comprised 20 percent of common air, and its properties were different from the rest of air. Priestley's dephlogisticated air was the component of common air that supported combustion.

Lavoisier proposed that combustion did not result from the loss of phlogiston, but from the combination of this pure air with metals. Lavoisier named this type of air "oxygen," which means "acid-former," but this turned out to be a misnomer. While it is true that the combination of sulfur, phosphorus, and other metals with oxygen leads to the formation of acids, such as sulfuric acid and phosphoric acid, not all acids contain oxygen. For example, hydrochloric acid consists only of the elements hydrogen and chloride. The addition of oxygen explained the increase in weight of the metals after burning. He named the remaining part of air "azote" (meaning "no life"). Today this is called nitrogen.

When Lavoisier reported these findings to the Academy of Sciences, he failed to mention Priestley's contribution. While he was brilliant at drawing conclusions from the experiments of others, he was quick to take all the credit for himself. He made this same gaffe after concluding that water was composed of hydrogen and oxygen.

In 1781, the English chemist Henry Cavendish, who was famous for discovering inflammable air (hydrogen), ascertained that the moisture that resulted following the explosive mixture of inflammable air and oxygen was plain water. Upon learning of this, Lavoisier hypothesized that water was not an element but was a compound whose components were the elements oxygen and inflammable air, which he named hydrogen (meaning "water-former"). He then performed experiments that supported his hypothesis. He was able to synthesize water using hydrogen and oxygen and then break it back down into its component parts, which proved to be hydrogen and oxygen. This conclusion that water was a compound gave Lavoisier the impetus to start attacking the phlogiston theory publicly and viciously.

By 1783, Lavoisier had fully presented his case against the phlogiston theory, declaring his support for the oxygen theory of combustion. The main points of his argument were logical conclusions based on facts and observations from his experiments. Common air was a mixture composed of at least two different gases. One of them was oxygen. This gas combined with metals during combustion and supported *respiration*. The other component of air, azote, did not support combustion or respiration. Metal calces were not elements, but were compounds composed of metals and oxygen. Oxygen logically explained all the changes that occurred. These ideas were summarized in a letter to the academy, "Reflections on Phlogiston,"

Claude-Louis Berthollet (1748–1822)

The book *Méthode de nomenclature chimique,* published in 1787, was indispensable for presenting a logical system for naming chemical compounds, the basis for the system used today. Substances were named based on the elements of which they were composed; thus, the names indicated what each compound contained. Three other inventive chemists collaborated with Lavoisier on this effort, including Claude-Louis Berthollet (1748–1822).

Berthollet was one of the first chemists to adopt Lavoisier's new antiphlogiston chemistry. Working as the director of a textile factory, he studied the process of bleaching. He determined that chlorine, discovered in 1774 by Carl Wilhelm Scheele, was an effective bleaching agent. Berthollet's belief in 1786. Many older scientists were resistant to accepting these changes, as it would require that the entire structure of chemistry be rebuilt from scratch. Lavoisier also realized this and set out to accomplish this task.

The Language of Chemistry Rewritten

From his research, Lavoisier realized that the term *element* needed redefining. He revived a definition originally proposed by Robert Boyle, who defined an element as a substance that cannot be further broken down by chemical means. Elements could combine with other elements to form compounds. This was not enough to satisfy him, however. In collaboration with French chemist Louis-Bernard Guyton de Morveau, who was struggling to write an encyclopedia entry about the history of chemistry, Lavoisier decided there was a need to revise the entire language of chemistry in light of the oxygen theory of combustion. They enlisted the help of two other French

that chlorine was an oxygen-containing compound rather than an element was incorrect, but his investigations on chlorine led to studies on potassium chlorate, which he found exploded when mixed with carbon. He also performed analyses on ammonia and determined its composition (NH_3).

Though he agreed with Lavoisier's oxygen theory of combustion, Berthollet did not believe that all acids contained oxygen, as Lavoisier did. Many common acids do, such as nitric acid (HNO_3) and sulfuric acid (H_2SO_4), but Berthollet's studies on prussic acid (now called hydrocyanic acid, HCN) demonstrated that it was not imperative that a substance contain oxygen in order to have acidic properties.

Berthollet is most famous for proposing, in 1803, what is now called the law of mass action. This law states that masses of reactants affect the speed of a chemical reaction. It took almost 75 years and the influence of physical chemistry before this idea was widely accepted. Berthollet incorrectly believed, however, that the masses of reactants affected the composition of the products.

tasks, such as sitting still, lifting a weight, and eating, while Lavoisier carefully monitored his oxygen intake, carbon dioxide output, pulse rate, and respiration rate. They discovered that more oxygen was consumed when working, and the subject's heartbeat and respiration rate increased. They also found that more oxygen was consumed at colder temperatures, supporting Lavoisier's hypothesis that animals generated body heat by respiration. These results were reported to the academy in 1790.

While Lavoisier's groundwork formed the foundation of modern chemistry, he contributed to other fields as well. He was an active member of the Agricultural Society of Paris and became a commissioner to agriculture. He owned a 1,200-acre farm on which he pioneered experimental farming by using the scientific method to improve crop yields and animal number. To examine his hypothesis that grain yield was related to the manure left behind by grazing animals, he increased the number of cattle roaming on the fields and also rotated crops. He kept very careful records and showed that his methods practically doubled grain yield every two years. In doing so, he opened up the field of scientific agriculture. He also made suggestions for greater efficiency in hospitals and prisons, as well as proposed banking reforms and new tax systems. He recommended that all children should be educated through secondary school. Many of his suggestions were ignored. At the time of his death he was standardizing the system for weights and measures. Today the metric system is used worldwide.

The Execution of Lavoisier

The French Revolution broke out in July of 1789. The French common people were angry with King Louis XVI, who kept raising their taxes. Lavoisier supported the Revolution in its early stages. He thought the people should have more say in how the government was run. However, as a member of the Ferme Générale, a tax collection agency, he became a target. The new leaders arrested all the tax collectors for charging excessive rates and withholding money owed to the government treasury.

One man who testified against Lavoisier was French journalist Jean-Paul Marat, who, interestingly, had previously authored a paper that Lavoisier criticized and whom Lavoisier had voted against in his application to the Academy of Sciences. Marat held a grudge and enacted his revenge by accusing Lavoisier of watering down commercial tobacco and smothering the city inhabitants with the wall surrounding Paris. When Lavoisier tried to defend himself, the Revolutionary Tribunal did not listen to him. They did not trust educated people and were anxious to be rid of all connections with the old government. They had found correspondence of Lavoisier with scientists from countries that were France's political enemies. When Lavoisier tried to explain that he was just a scientist, the judge replied that the republic had no need for scientists. After a mock 15-minute trial, he was sentenced to death at the guillotine. On May 8, 1794, Antoine Lavoisier lost his head, and the world lost a brilliant scientist.

At the age of 50, the founder of modern chemistry was beheaded. He was still peaking mentally. Yet during his short life he was able to launch a revolution in the field of chemistry. He furnished chemists with a logical, easy-to-understand language by which to communicate, and this allowed his new ideas to spread rapidly. He published the first chemistry textbook, which disseminated the information necessary to permit further *expansion* of the ideas he birthed and was a standard for decades. Lavoisier demonstrated the importance of accurate and precise measurement in performing chemical experiments. He explained the process of combustion in terms of oxygen and removed the hindrance of phlogiston from the progress of chemical research. He reorganized the jumbled mess of random chemical facts and turned them into a true science.

CHRONOLOGY

1743	Antoine Lavoisier is born in Paris, France, on August 26
1754–63	Attends Collège des Quatre-Nations, obtaining a baccalaureate in law
1763–66	Accompanies Jean-Étienne Guettard on a geological tour of France
1765	Submits his first paper on gypsum to Academy of Sciences

1766	Earns a medal in a competition for improving street lighting in Paris
1768	Joins the Ferme Générale and proves water cannot be transmutated into earth
1772–73	Shows that metals burn by absorbing a component from air
1774	Publishes first book, *Opuscules physiques et chimiques* (Essays physical and chemical)
1775	Confirms Priestley's result that mercury calx gives off "pure air" when broken down and becomes a commissioner for the Royal Gunpowder Administration
1775–83	Collects and presents evidence supporting the oxygen theory of combustion and refuting the phlogiston theory
1781–84	Lavoisier performs calorimeter experiments and studies animal heat with Laplace, leading to his conclusion that respiration is simply slow combustion. Shows water is a compound of hydrogen and oxygen
1786	Writes "Reflections on Phlogiston," summarizing the oxygen theory of combustion
1787	Copublishes *Méthode de nomenclature chimique* (Method of chemical nomenclature) with Claude-Louis Berthollet, Louis-Bernard Guyton de Morveau, and Antoine Fourcroy
1789	Publishes *An Elementary Treatise of Chemistry* and founds the journal *Annales de Chimie* (Annals of chemistry)
1790	Reports findings on human respiration
1791	Begins to reform the system of weights and measures
1794	Is executed by the guillotine, at age 50, in Paris, on May 8

FURTHER READING

Allaby, Michael, and Derek Gjertsen, eds. *Makers of Science.* Vol. 1. New York: Oxford University Press, 2002. Chronological biographies of influential scientists. Includes political and social settings as well as scientific achievements.

"Antoine Lavoisier." Chemical Heritage Foundation, 2000. Available online. URL: http://www.chemheritage.org/EducationalServices/chemach/fore/all.html. Accessed February 1, 2005. Part of the chemical achievers biographical profile series aimed at middle and high school students.

Gillispie, Charles C., ed. *Dictionary of Scientific Biography*. Vol. 8. New York: Scribner, 1970–76. Good source for facts concerning personal background and scientific accomplishments but assumes basic knowledge of science.

Grey, Vivian. *The Chemist Who Lost His Head*. New York: Coward-McCann, 1982. Recounts Lavoisier's life, accomplishments, and the events that led to his execution. Appropriate for middle school students.

Meadows, Jack. *The Great Scientists: The Story of Science Told Through the Lives of Twelve Landmark Figures*. New York: Oxford University Press, 1987. Brief biographies of 12 high-profile scientists and the development of science as influenced by social forces. Colorful illustrations.

Poole, Lynn, and Gray Poole. *Scientists Who Changed the World*. New York: Dodd, Mead, and Company, 1963. Easy-to-read profiles of the scientists who made a dozen revolutionary discoveries.

Saari, Peggy, and Stephen Allison, eds. *The Lives and Works of 150 Scientists*. Vol. 2. Detroit, Mich.: U*X*L, 1996. Alphabetically arranged introductions to the contributions of scientists from a variety of fields. Intended for middle school students.

John Dalton

3

(1766–1844)

John Dalton formulated the chemical atomic theory. (*Science Photo Library/Photo Researchers, Inc.*)

The Chemical Atomic Theory

The Greek philosopher Democritus was the first to use the word *atom*, meaning "indivisible," to describe the smallest unit of matter. Today an atom is defined as the smallest component of an element that retains the chemical properties of that element. Atoms combine to form compounds. The smallest physical unit of a compound is a molecule. These concepts are introduced at the beginning of chemistry courses because all of chemistry is defined in

The Manchester Literary and Philosophical Society

A few years prior, Dalton had seemed unhappy with his career and his life. He complained that he was not earning enough money by teaching to get married and start a family. He even considered changing careers and going into law or medicine. On the advice of respected relatives and Robinson, however, he kept on teaching. After an expected period of adjustment to teaching courses at the college level in Manchester, he found that a career in teaching permitted him to indulge in additional activities. He continued recording meteorological observations and found himself becoming very interested in weather and atmospheric phenomena. He sought out colleagues that shared his intellectual interests and became a member of the Manchester Literary and Philosophical Society in 1794. The members met regularly to discuss literature and recent scientific advancements. Dalton became very involved with this society, serving as its secretary (1800), vice president (1808), and president (1817 until the time of his death). On an irregular basis, papers presented to the society were published in the society's *Memoirs*. Over his lifetime Dalton presented 117 papers to the society, and 52 were published in the *Memoirs*. The environment in Manchester was quite fulfilling; Dalton was able to utilize the resources afforded by the larger city and academic environment to develop his personal intellectual interests. He never married, but he made many friends and was active in the community and contributed his time and abilities to the Society of Friends.

Though he performed well at New College, Dalton began his own prosperous private tutoring business while in Manchester. Eight or nine pupils visited each day to be instructed in the subjects of mathematics, natural philosophy, and grammar. When he was dissatisfied with the selection of textbooks for teaching grammar, he wrote his own successful text, *Elements of English Grammar*, published in 1801. In 1800, he resigned his position at New College, which was having financial difficulties, and supported himself for the remainder of his life by privately tutoring students. The Literary and Philosophical Society allowed Dalton the use of some rooms at their headquarters for teaching and research. He researched scientific topics that fascinated him.

Daltonism and Atmospheric Sciences

In 1794, Dalton presented his first scientific paper, titled "Extraordinary Facts Relating to the Vision of Colours, with Observations," to the Literary and Philosophical Society. Both of the Dalton brothers suffered what today is commonly known as red-green color blindness, sometimes called *daltonism*. Individuals who suffer this genetic disorder are unable to distinguish the colors red and green. John had observed that he saw colors differently than other people while studying botany a few years earlier. He collected information from other people with a similar disability and offered a hypothesis explaining the affliction. He thought the aqueous medium in the eyeballs of afflicted individuals was bluish in color; thus, it would absorb red light rays and prevent the person from seeing the color red. Dalton was typically a stubborn proponent of his own beliefs. He made arrangements for his eyeballs to be dissected upon his death in order to prove his hypothesis. Unfortunately, he was incorrect, but his original paper on the matter was pioneering, as it was the first scientific accounting of the disease. In 1995, DNA analysis from his preserved eyeball confirmed Dalton had the gene causing deuteranopia, the most common form of color blindness.

In *Meteorological Observations and Essays*, Dalton had begun a discussion on the behavior of gases. Over the next few years he expanded his interests and studied rain, evaporation, water vapor, and heat. He did not subscribe to the popular belief that air was a compound but believed it was rather a mixture of several different gases. He published this idea in 1801, in the *Journal of Natural Philosophy, Chemistry, and the Arts*, known thereafter as *Nicholson's Journal*. The papers Dalton presented to the Manchester Literary and Philosophical Society following the *Nicholson's Journal* article proposed that the total pressure of a gaseous mixture was the sum of the independent pressures of each individual gas in the mixture. In other words, if a mixture contained two gases named A and B, the total pressure exerted by the mixture was the sum of the pressure exerted by gas A plus the pressure exerted by the gas B. Today we call this Dalton's law, or the law of partial pressures. He also reported that all elastic fluids (gases) expand by the same quantity of heat. At a constant pressure the volume of a gas increased or decreased with temperature. This is referred to as Charles's law, since it was discovered previously (though unpublished) by the French physicist Jacques Charles. Many scientists thought this was hogwash, including Gough, but Dalton's stubborn scientific ego refused to accept the criticism. He was determined to provide more experimental evidence supporting his ideas.

As a result, in late 1802 Dalton read a paper to the Literary and Philosophical Society in which he discussed the composition of the atmosphere. He also emphasized that gases such as CO_2 were absorbed into liquids (such as air) by mechanical forces, not by chemical means. He defined the law of multiple proportions, stating that when the same two elements form a series of compounds, the ratio of masses of each element in the compounds for a given mass of any other element is a small whole number. For example, methane (CH_4) and ethylene (C_2H_4) are both composed of carbon and hydrogen, but experimental evidence showed that twice as much hydrogen combined with a constant amount of carbon in methane than in ethylene. The ratios of carbon to hydrogen are 1:4 and 1:2, respectively.

The Tiniest Parts

Dalton continued his solubility studies, and in early 1803, he showed that when a heavy and a light gas mixed together, they spontaneously diffused and stayed that way. This suggested that particles of a gas only repelled other similar particles of the same gas, leading Dalton to start thinking of atoms as the smallest indivisible bits of matter, not only in gases, but also in liquids and solids. The concept of atoms as indivisible particles of matter was not revolutionary per se, but Dalton thought to define atoms by their weights. Originally he believed that particles of all gases were the same size but then thought, why should some particles specifically repel only other similar particles? He decided that all the atoms of a specific element must have equal weights, while atoms of different elements have different weights. For example, all carbon atoms had the same size and atomic weight as each other but different sizes and weights than nitrogen atoms.

Because atoms are so minuscule (a single hydrogen atom weighs approximately 1.67×10^{-24} grams), it was impossible to determine the weight of individual atoms, so Dalton invented a relative system. He assigned hydrogen, the lightest known element, an atomic weight of 1, and then atomic weights of all other elements were reported relative to the weight of hydrogen. These could be determined experimentally. For example, since hydrogen combined with eight times its own weight in oxygen to form water, he assigned oxygen an atomic weight of 8. He incorrectly assumed the combining ratio of hydrogen to oxygen was 1:1. Today chemists know that two atoms of hydrogen combine with a single atom of oxygen to form water, H_2O, but Dalton had no way of knowing the ratios by which atoms combined, so he assumed the simplest possible ratio. Also today, because weight is technically the measure of heaviness of an object and mass is the total amount of matter in an object, it is more accurate to talk of *atomic mass*. In a paper presented to the Manchester Literary and Philosophical Society in late 1803, "The Absorption of Gases by Water and Other Liquids," Dalton included the first table of relative atomic weights.

Dalton suggested compounds were formed by the combination of atoms of different elements. Later, the Italian chemist Amedeo Avogadro said that atoms of the same element could combine to form compounds, just like atoms of different elements. Dalton stated that atoms always combined to form simple ratios, such as 1:1 or 1:2. These ratios were predictable and constant for all molecules of the same compound. (The term *molecules* was suggested later.)

A New System

In 1807, Dalton gave a series of lectures in Edinburgh and Glasgow, Scotland, to present the above ideas in a coherent chemical atomic theory. The content of these lectures was really a preview of his book, *A New System of Chemical Philosophy*, the first part of which was published in 1808. The second part was published in 1810. Much of this seminal work was devoted to heat, but the work also delineated his theory on the particulate nature of matter, the chemical atomic theory. The atomic theory pronounced that central particles, or atoms, of homogenous bodies all had equal weights that differed from those of different elements. Dalton included a discussion of the constitution of bodies as sets of rules for combining elements into compounds. He also stated that central particles could neither be created nor destroyed any easier than an entire planet could be created or destroyed. When new materials are created, old combinations of particles are simply remixed into new combinations. The idea that atoms combine chemically in simple ratios to create molecules

DALTON'S NOTATION

Hydrogen	⊙	Copper	©
Nitrogen	⊕	Lead	ⓛ
Carbon	●	Water	⊙○
Sulfur	⊕	Ammonia	⊙⊕
Phosphorus	⊗	Olefiant	⊙●
Alumina	⊙	Carbonic oxide	○●
Soda	⊕	Carbonic acid	○●○
Pot ash	⊕		
Oxygen	○	Sulfuric acid	⊕

Dalton created arbitrary symbols to represent atoms of different elements and to pictorially describe the composition of different compounds. He was incorrect about the proportions of elements in some of the compounds.

Baron Jöns Jakob Berzelius (1779–1848)

The name of Jöns Jakob Berzelius (1779–1848) may be most familiar for his idea of symbolizing the chemical elements with letters. He used the first letter of the Latin name of each element and if two elements shared the first letter, he used the first two letters. His symbols were easy to learn and recognize; for example, oxygen was *O*, nitrogen was *N*, and calcium *Ca*. Berzelius dominated the field of chemistry in the early 1800s.

As a supporter of Dalton's atomic theory, Berzelius recognized the importance of determining the accurate atomic weights of the elements. From 1807 to 1817, he analyzed over 2,000 compounds made of 43 (which Dalton confusingly referred to as "compound atoms") was also articulated. The text reviewed Dalton's law of multiple proportions and the law of constant composition, which was proposed by the French chemist Joseph Louis Proust in 1799 and stated that the relative masses of elements are fixed in a pure chemical compound. The major contribution of the *New System* was the proposal of a method of establishing relative atomic weights from chemical data of composition percentages. Most famous chemists quickly adopted Dalton's *New System* philosophies. The second volume did not come out until 1827 and was not nearly as popular as the first. This may be due to the material being outdated by the time it was finally published.

Dalton used a system of chemical notation involving open circles with different letters or symbols inside of them. This made it easier to write out chemical reactions and revealed a bit of information on the mechanics of each reaction; for example, the number of atoms of each element in a compound. When the Swedish chemist Baron Jöns Jakob Berzelius proposed a logical alphabetical system of chemical symbols, the same system that is widely used at present,

elements, and in 1828, he published a table of the most accurate atomic weights of the time. He discovered three new elements—selenium, silicon, and thorium—and with the Swedish geologist Wilhelm Hisinger, discovered a fourth, cerium, that was also discovered by the German chemist Martin Heinrich Klaproth. He later coined the term *isomer* to indicate a chemical compound that has the same formula but different chemical or physical properties than another compound. He also proposed the term *allotrope* to describe elements that occur in more than one form and differ in chemical or physical properties but not in the kind of atoms of which they are composed.

Berzelius proposed a theory to explain why atoms join together in fixed proportions to make compounds. He suggested that all compounds contain atoms that are positively charged and negatively charged, joined together by an electrochemical reaction in fixed proportions. This dualistic theory never became widely accepted.

CHRONOLOGY

1766	John Dalton is born in Eaglesfield, England, on September 5 or 6
1778	Takes over the local Quaker school
1781	Moves to Kendall to tutor at the Quaker school
1785	Becomes a joint principal at the Kendal school
1787	Begins keeping a meteorological journal
1793	Publishes his first book, *Meteorological Observations and Essays,* and starts teaching at New College in Manchester
1794	Joins the Manchester Literary and Philosophical Society and reads his first scientific paper on color blindness
1800	Resigns from New College
1801	Publishes *Elements of English Grammar* and his theory of mixed gases in *Nicholson's Journal*
1802–05	Develops the atomic theory
1803	Presents a paper with the first table of atomic weights
1807	Presents the ideas comprising the chemical atomic theory at lectures in Scotland
1808–10	Publishes the first volume of *A New System of Chemical Philosophy*
1827	Publishes the second volume of *A New System of Chemical Philosophy*
1844	Dies in Manchester at age 79, on July 27

FURTHER READING

Gillispie, Charles C., ed. *Dictionary of Scientific Biography.* Vol. 3. New York: Scribner, 1970–76. Good source for facts concerning personal background and scientific accomplishments but assumes basic knowledge of science.

Holmyard, E. J. *Chemistry to the Time of Dalton.* London: Oxford University Press, 1925. Old, but useful in explaining the development of premodern chemistry.

"John Dalton." Chemical Heritage Foundation, 2000. Available online. URL: http://www.chemheritage.org/EducationalServices/chemach/ppt/jd.html. Accessed February 2, 2005. Part of the chemical achievers biographical profile series aimed at middle and high school students.

McDonnell, John J. *The Concept of an Atom from Democritus to John Dalton.* Lewiston, New York: Edwin Mellen Press, 1991. The story of the development of the concept of the atom beginning in ancient Greece.

Patterson, Elizabeth C. *John Dalton and the Atomic Theory: The Biography of a Natural Philosopher.* Garden City, N.Y.: Doubleday and Company, 1982. Describes Dalton's life in the context of 19th-century England and the investigations that led to his new understanding of matter. Written for adult readers.

Saari, Peggy, and Stephen Allison, eds. *The Lives and Works of 150 Scientists.* Vol. 1. Detroit, Mich.: U*X*L, 1996. Alphabetically arranged introductions to the contributions of scientists from a variety of fields. Intended for middle school students.

Simmons, John. *The Scientific 100: A Ranking of the Most Influential Scientists, Past and Present.* Secaucus, N.J.: Carol Publishing Group, 1996. Rankings of 100 broadly ranging scientists with descriptions of their achievements.

Dmitry Mendeleyev

4

(1834-1907)

Dmitry Mendeleyev's development of the periodic table of the elements brought organization to the chaotic field of inorganic chemistry. *(Science Photo Library/Photo Researchers, Inc.)*

The Periodic Table of the Elements

At the beginning of the 19th century, the English chemist John Dalton proposed the atomic theory of matter. The idea that all matter was composed of atoms and their different combinations soon became widely accepted. Chemists learned to differentiate between elements and compounds and characterized 63 different elements by midcentury. Several chemists pursued the defining relationships among the chemical elements in an attempt to bring organization to the growing list. The search for whatever naturally governed the outwardly random list seemed in vain until one man established the unifying principle of atomic weight. The result was perhaps the most important scientific construct to withstand the test of time—the *periodic table* of the elements. In discovering periodic dependence upon atomic weight and developing the periodic table, the Siberian chemist Dmitry Mendeleyev transformed the seemingly nebulous subject of inorganic chemistry into an organized, methodical scientific field.

Tragic Beginnings

Dmitry Ivanovich Mendeleyev was born on February 8, 1834, in Tobolsk, in western Siberia. He was the youngest of at least 14 children (records disagree as to the actual number). His father, Ivan Pavlovich Mendeleyev, lost his job teaching Russian literature at the gymnasium after developing blinding cataracts when Dmitry was very young. His mother, Maria Dmitryevna Kornileva, worked to support the large family by reviving an abandoned glass manufacturing factory. Dmitry entered the Tobolsk gymnasium at age seven and enjoyed history, mathematics, and physics. A brother-in-law who had been exiled to Siberia for revolutionary activities in Moscow taught science to Dmitry. When Dmitry was a teenager, his father died and his mother's factory burned down. He was only an average student, but his mother was determined that he have a chance for success. She took him by horseback to enroll him at the University of Moscow, but Siberians were prohibited from admission. She took him to St. Petersburg and, in 1850, enrolled him at the Main Pedagogical Institute to study physics and mathematics. She died a few months later, leaving Dmitry fiercely determined to prove that her efforts to obtain an education for her youngest son were not in vain.

Mendeleyev graduated from the teacher's college in 1855, having developed a predilection for chemistry and research. His dissertation, titled "Isomorphism in Connection with Other Relations of Form to Composition," examined the effect of chemical composition on the *crystal* structures of certain substances and was published in the *Mining Journal* in 1856. After graduation, he obtained a teaching position in Odessa, where he carried on with his research and supplemented his income by writing articles on education and on chemical applications to industry. In September 1856, Mendeleyev received a master's degree from the University of St. Petersburg. His dissertation, "Specific Volumes," explored the relationship of chemical and crystallographic properties of substances with their specific volumes.

Structure-Function Relationships of Chemical Substances

After lecturing for several years, Mendeleyev resumed his studies in chemistry with chemist Robert Bunsen at the University of Heidelberg, in Germany. During the period 1859–60, he researched the nature of solutions and the expansion of liquids by heating. In 1860, he discovered the phenomenon of *critical temperature*, the temperature at which a liquid and its vapor exist at equilibrium. At the critical temperature, a gas may be turned into a liquid by the application of pressure alone. Above the critical temperature, a gas cannot be liquefied, no matter how much pressure is applied. The Irish chemist Thomas Andrews is sometimes given credit for discovering this phenomenon, but Mendeleyev's work predates the work of Andrews.

An important meeting, the First International Chemical Congress, took place at Karlsruhe, Germany, in 1860. Mendeleyev had risen to become one of Russia's leading scientists, and the government selected him to attend. The standardization of the methods for determining atomic weights was one of the items on the agenda, as the current list contained many contradictions. At the meeting, an Italian chemist named Stanislao Cannizzaro circulated a syllabus that showed how Amedeo Avogadro's hypothesis furnished an unambiguous method for determining atomic and molecular weights. Avogadro (1776–1856) was an Italian physicist and chemist who, in 1811, announced that all gases contain the same number of particles per unit volume at the same temperature and pressure. Particles were either individual atoms or molecules. His hypothesis was largely ignored until Cannizzaro revived it at the congress. Once resurrected, this principle of equivalence allowed the elements to be accurately weighed. *Avogadro's number,* the number of atoms or molecules present in an amount of a substance that has a mass equal to its atomic weight in grams, is named in his honor. The value of Avogadro's number equals 6.02×10^{23}. Little did Mendeleyev know of the significance that the concept of atomic weights would have in his future.

In 1861, Mendeleyev returned to St. Petersburg and became a professor of chemistry at the Technological Institute. He continued his research and published several articles. The same year he returned he also published an award-winning textbook, *Organic Chemistry*. At the urging of his sister, he married Feozva Nikitichna Leshcheva in 1862. They had two children before separating. In 1865, he earned his doctorate degree in chemistry from the University of St. Petersburg by defending his dissertation, "On the Compounds of Alcohol with Water." He was appointed a professor of general chemistry at the University of St. Petersburg in 1867.

Until this point, Mendeleyev's research focused on the relationship between the chemical or physical properties of substances and chemical composition. All matter is composed of atoms, the smallest particles of an element that retain its chemical properties. An element is a substance that cannot be broken down further; elements are composed of single atom types. Atoms have a central nucleus that contains the subatomic particles called protons and neutrons. Electrons, a third type of subatomic particle, surround the nucleus. The electrons are often depicted as a continuous cloud since they are constantly moving, but the movement of individual electrons is restricted by the electron *shell* that they occupy. Each shell can hold a specific

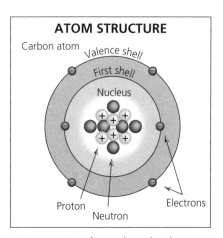

ATOM STRUCTURE

Carbon atom
Valence shell
First shell
Nucleus
Proton
Neutron
Electrons

Atoms consist of a nucleus that houses protons and neutrons surrounded by an electron cloud. Negatively charged electrons orbit the nucleus in distinct energy levels called electron shells. In a carbon atom, two electrons occupy the first electron shell, and four electrons occupy the valence shell.

and limited number of electrons. The innermost shell of an atom can hold two electrons, the second and third shells can hold up to eight electrons, and the fourth and fifth shell can hold up to 18 electrons. The shells are filled successively. If an atom has 12 electrons, the first shell would contain two (the maximum number it can hold), the second shell would contain eight (the maximum number it can hold), and the third shell would only contain two. Atoms with filled outer shells are more stable; thus, when forming a chemical bond with another atom, the outer shell may gain or lose electrons in an attempt to fill its outermost shell. The *valence* of an atom is the number of electrons it must gain or lose in order to fill its outer shell. The valence equals the number of single bonds that an atom may form. Chemical properties of elements are dictated by the number of electrons contained in their outermost shells, or *valence shells*. Years spent examining the structure-function relationship of chemical substances prepared Mendeleyev for a pioneering development.

Finally, a Unifying Principle

While teaching at the University of St. Petersburg, Mendeleyev wrote a very successful two-volume chemistry textbook, *The Principles of Chemistry* (1868–70). While conducting research in preparation for writing the text, he became interested in the relationships among the chemical elements. The physical states of the pure elements differed: solid, liquid, or gas. Some of the elements were hard and others were soft. They were different colors and exhibited a variety of chemical properties. Yet Mendeleyev was convinced there was an underlying logical connection and was determined to uncover it. He searched for a clear and logical manner to present the elements to his readers. Mendeleyev proceeded by creating a deck of cards, with each card representing one of the 63 known elements. The cards also included other information such as valence and other chemical and physical properties.

Mendeleyev arranged and rearranged his cards according to the properties listed on them. Then one day he awoke from an afternoon nap with an epiphany. He realized that atomic weight was the most logical characteristic by which to categorize the elements. Atomic weight is the mass of an atom and is largely dependent on

The Periodic Table of the Elements

The periodic table is a convenient means for introducing the chemical elements. (A modern periodic table of the elements may be found at the back of this book.) The recurrence of chemical properties of the elements when arranged by *atomic number* is referred to as *periodic law*. The elements are represented by alphabetical symbols inside squares that are arranged into seven rows. The atomic number of each element is listed above the chemical symbol. The concept of atomic number, or number of protons in the nucleus of an atom, was not developed until 1914 by the English physicist Henry Moseley. Mendeleyev used atomic weight, which today is more correctly referred to as *atomic mass*. Though atomic mass is related to atomic number in that the number of protons constitutes a significant proportion of the total mass, atomic number later proved to be a better factor for assigning placement in the periodic table. Atomic number increases in distinct increments with the addition of single protons, and the table was modified accordingly so that now the elements are identified by atomic number. The atomic mass, or the average relative mass of an atom compared to that of carbon-12, is listed below each symbol.

Each horizontal row in the table is called a *period*. The first period contains only two elements. The second and third periods have eight elements, and the fourth and fifth periods each contain 18 elements. Each vertical column of the table is referred to as a group, and the elements it contains share similar chemical properties. Several groups are

the number of protons and neutrons an atom contains. When he set out the cards by increasing atomic weights, he noticed that a recurring pattern emerged: every eighth element seemed to share similar properties. He laid the cards out in the form of a table, also given names; for example, the first group (with the exception of hydrogen) is called the alkali metals. All of the alkali metals are very reactive and easily lose an electron to form positively charged ions. The last group, number 18, is called the "noble gases." These elements all have completely filled valence shells and are unreactive.

Clusters of elements that do not necessarily belong to the same group but share some similar properties are physically located near one another. For example, the metallic elements are all capable of conducting electricity, are malleable, shiny, and are solid at room temperature (with the exception of mercury). All the metals are clustered on the left side of the periodic table. The nonmetals, such as carbon, phosphorus, and sulfur, are located on the right side of the table. Placement in the periodic table also allows predictions to be made concerning chemical reactivity. To illustrate, metals and nonmetals, located on opposite sides of the periodic table, usually combine to form ionic compounds.

Another periodic trend is size. As one moves down a group, the size of the atoms of those elements increases. Size decreases as one moves from the left to the right across a period.

The number of electrons in the outermost shell, called the valence shell, is also a periodic property. The number of electron shells an atom contains equals the period in which the element is found; for example, magnesium is in period three, and it has three electron shells. As one moves from left to right across a period, there is one more electron in the valence shell. For magnesium, there are two electrons in the outermost shell, and it is found in group two. The number of electrons in the valence shell determines the combining power of that element. One can therefore predict chemical properties based on the position of an element within the periodic table or the group to which it belongs.

beginning a new row after every eight elements. The elements in each resulting column shared similar properties. Interruptions existed in the pattern, however. When a reported atomic weight resulted in questionable placement with respect to an element's

но въ ней, мнѣ кажется, уже ясно выражается примѣнимость вы-
ставляемаго мною начала ко всей совокупности элементовъ, пай
которыхъ извѣстенъ съ достовѣрностію. На этотъ разъ я и желалъ
преимущественно найдти общую систему элементовъ. Вотъ этотъ
опытъ:

			Ti=50	Zr=90	?=180.
			V=51	Nb=94	Ta=182.
			Cr=52	Mo=96	W=186.
			Mn=55	Rh=104,4	Pt=197,4
			Fe=56	Ru=104,4	Ir=198.
		Ni=Co=59		Pl=106,6,	Os=199.
H=1			Cu=63,4	Ag=108	Hg=200.
	Be=9,4	Mg=24	Zn=65,2	Cd=112	
	B=11	Al=27,4	?=68	Ur=116	Au=197?
	C=12	Si=28	?=70	Sn=118	
	N=14	P=31	As=75	Sb=122	Bi=210
	O=16	S=32	Se=79,4	Te=128?	
	F=19	Cl=35,5	Br=80	I=127	
Li=7	Na=23	K=39	Rb=85,4	Cs=133	Tl=204
		Ca=40	Sr=87,6	Ba=137	Pb=207.
		?=45	Ce=92		
		?Er=56	La=94		
		?Yt=60	Di=95		
		?In=75,6	Th=118?		

а потому приходится въ разныхъ рядахъ имѣть различное измѣненіе разностей,
чего нѣтъ въ главныхъ числахъ предлагаемой таблицы. Или же придется предпо-
лагать при составленіи системы очень много недостающихъ членовъ. То и
другое мало выгодно. Мнѣ кажется притомъ, наиболѣе естественнымъ составить
кубическую систему (предлагаемая есть плоскостная), но и попытки для ея образо-
ванія не повели къ надлежащимъ результатамъ. Слѣдующія двѣ попытки могутъ по-
казать то разнообразіе сопоставленій, какое возможно при допущеніи основнаго
начала, высказаннаго въ этой статьѣ.

Li	Na	K	Cu	Rb	Ag	Cs	—	Tl
7	23	39	63,4	85,4	108	133		204
Be	Mg	Ca	Zn	Sr	Cd	Ba	—	Pb
B	Al	—	—	—	Ur	—	—	Bi?
C	Si	Ti	—	Zr	Sn	—	—	—
N	P	V	As	Nb	Sb	—	Ta	—
O	S	—	Se	—	Te	—	W	—
F	Cl	—	Br	—	J	—	—	—
19	35,5	58	80	190	127	160	190	220.

Mendeleyev published his first periodic table of the elements in 1869. *(Library of Congress, Prints and Photographs Division [LC-USZ62-95277])* properties, Mendeleyev positioned the element according to its properties. For example, beryllium was thought to have an atomic weight of 14, but Mendeleyev presumed it to fit better in group two rather than group 15. He correctly predicted the weight was nine, and placed it accordingly. In the early 1900s, the English physicist Henry Moseley determined the correct atomic weights for several of the elements, proving Mendeleyev was very intuitive.

Despite overcoming the difficulty of approximated atomic weights, other imperfections in the table persisted. In order to maintain the periodicity, Mendeleyev was forced to assume that several elements were missing, that is, not yet discovered. He was struck in particular by gaps in the group containing boron and aluminum. Leaving three spaces in that group blank, he arranged the other elements according to their chemical properties, predicting that the missing elements would be discovered in the future. Mendeleyev then boldly predicted not only their atomic weights but other properties, including specific densities, specific heats, and the compounds they would form. Many scientists were skeptical and perhaps offended by Mendeleyev's temerity, but the missing elements—gallium, scandium, and germanium—were discovered in 1875, 1879, and 1886, respectively, verifying all of Mendeleyev's predictions.

An Ambitious Activist

Mendeleyev was an ambitious man who used his talents not only to advance the field of chemistry but to promote the education of Russia's citizens and help improve their economy. In 1868, he assisted in founding the Russian Chemical Society (now the Mendeleyev Russian Chemical Society). The goal of this organization is to unite chemists working in the fields of scientific research, industry, and education and to further the progress of chemistry, the chemical industry, and the teaching of chemistry in Russia. Every four years, in conjunction with the Russian Academy of Sciences, this same organization hosts the Mendeleyev Congress on General and Applied Chemistry and honors an outstanding chemist with the Golden Mendeleyev Medal.

In March of 1869, Mendeleyev's periodic table and the principles defining his periodic law were presented at a Russian Chemical Society meeting in a paper titled "Relation of the Properties to the Atomic Weights of the Elements." In 1871, he published his predictions about the three missing elements in the *Journal of the Russian Chemical Society*. A summary of his paper was published in German, making it more accessible to other scientists.

In 1876, Mendeleyev married Anna Ivanova Popov, with whom he shared the remainder of his life. Since he was not yet divorced from his first wife, this union caused him to become a bigamist. The czar excused Mendeleyev from prosecution for bigamy due to the prestige he brought Russia. Mendeleyev and his second wife had four children together.

Outside of his chemical research and writings, Mendeleyev strived to improve the economy of Russia. He promoted improved manufacturing, agriculture, trade, and the mining of coal, oil, and iron. Mendeleyev traveled to the United States in 1876 to learn about the petroleum industry, which he was working to develop in Russia. He was unimpressed with the lack of scientific interest and believed the U.S. petroleum industry was more concerned with quantity than product quality. Mendeleyev also criticized the Russian government for allowing their own oil resources to be exploited by foreign interests. The government did not welcome Mendeleyev's outspokenness, and they ignored his useful suggestions on how to improve the industry.

As a political activist, Mendeleyev publicly spoke in support of human rights. Though he had been elected a corresponding member of the St. Petersburg Academy of Sciences in 1876, his application for extraordinary membership was denied in 1880 due to his "threatening" humanitarian and democratic tendencies. He was forced to resign his professorship at the University of St. Petersburg in 1890, after personally delivering a petition from students who were protesting unjust conditions to the Ministry of Education. In 1893, Mendeleyev was appointed director of the Central Board of Weights and Measures. In this position, he helped update and regulate Russia's weights-and-measures system.

An Element in His Honor

After gallium, scandium, and germanium were discovered, Mendeleyev's ideas about periodic law became more widespread. Highly respected, he received the Davy medal from the Royal Society of London in 1882 and the Copley medal in 1905. In 1894, Oxford and Cambridge Universities conferred honorary doctorate degrees on him. Later in life, Mendeleyev suffered from cataracts. He died of pneumonia on February 2, 1907, and was buried in St. Petersburg. Hundreds of admiring students and colleagues marched in his funeral procession, carrying with them a periodic table of the elements.

Mendeleyev asserted that the chemical elements were in periodic dependence upon their atomic weights. From this intuitive notion, he introduced a comprehensible means to classify all the elements and relate them to one another. His system bestowed to chemists the power of prediction about new and undiscovered elements. The convenient method of displaying the elements that Mendeleyev proposed is still used today to introduce the chemical elements to beginning chemistry students, and modernized copies of the periodic table of the elements are posted across chemistry classrooms worldwide. Though other 19th-century scientists attempted to classify the chemical elements using atomic weight as a defining measure, Mendeleyev presented the most understandable and consistent scheme. He also was the only one bold enough to make accurate predictions about undiscovered elements based on his system of organization, and therefore he deserves the credit.

In 1955, three chemists at the University of California at Berkeley artificially produced an element with an atomic number of 101. This element was named mendelevium, honoring the brilliant chemist in perpetuity.

CHRONOLOGY

1834	Dmitry Mendeleyev is born in Tobolsk, Siberia, on February 8
1850–55	Attends a training college for teachers, the Main Pedagogical Institute, in St. Petersburg

1856	Publishes "Isomorphism in Connection with Other Relations of Form to Composition" in the *Mining Journal,* receives a master's degree in chemistry from the University of St. Petersburg, and becomes a chemistry lecturer
1859–60	Studies chemistry with Robert Bunsen at the University of Heidelberg, in Germany
1860	Discovers the phenomenon of critical temperature and participates in the International Chemical Congress in Karlsruhe
1861	Becomes a professor at the Technological Institute in St. Petersburg and publishes a textbook, *Organic Chemistry*
1865	Receives a doctorate degree in chemistry from the University of St. Petersburg
1867–90	Works as a professor of general chemistry at the University of St. Petersburg
1868	Publishes the first volume of *The Principles of Chemistry,* which went through eight editions during his lifetime, and helps found the Russian Chemical Society
1869	Discovery of periodic law is presented to the Russian Chemical Society in March
1870	Publishes the second volume of *The Principles of Chemistry*
1871	Publishes his predictions about undiscovered elements in the *Journal of the Russian Chemical Society*
1875	French chemist Lecoq de Boisbaudran discovers the element gallium, one of the elements Mendeleyev predicted was missing
1879	Swedish chemists Lars Nilson and Per Cleve discover and identify, respectively, the element scandium, the second missing element predicted by Mendeleyev
1886	German chemist Clemens Winkler discovers the element germanium, the last missing element predicted by Mendeleyev

1893–07	Serves as director of the Central Board of Weights and Measures
1907	Dies of pneumonia in St. Petersburg, on February 2
1956	Element 101, mendelevium, is named in honor of Mendeleyev

FURTHER READING

Adler, Robert E. *Science Firsts: From the Creation of Science to the Science of Creation.* New York: John Wiley, 2002. Stories of 35 landmark scientific discoveries including scientific and historical contexts.

"Dmitry Mendeleyev." Chemical Heritage Foundation, 2000. Available online. URL: http://www.chemheritage.org/explore/matter-Mendeleev.html. Accessed February 2, 2005. Part of the chemical achievers biographical profile series aimed at middle and high school students.

Gillispie, Charles C., ed. *Dictionary of Scientific Biography.* Vol. 9. New York: Scribner, 1970–76. Good source for facts concerning personal background and scientific accomplishments but assumes basic knowledge of science.

Horvitz, Leslie Alan. *Eureka! Scientific Breakthroughs that Changed the World.* New York: John Wiley, 2002. Explores the events and thought processes that led 12 great minds to their eureka moments.

Scientists and Inventors. New York: Macmillan, 1998. Brief profiles of the lives and works of more than 100 notable scientists, written for juvenile readers.

Strathern, Paul. *Mendeleyev's Dream: The Quest for the Elements.* New York: Thomas Dunne Books/St. Martin's Press, 2000. Uses Mendeleyev's accomplishment to reveal the history of chemistry.

Irving Langmuir

(1881–1957)

Irving Langmuir was awarded the Nobel Prize in chemistry in 1932 for his advancements in the field of surface chemistry. (© *The Nobel Foundation*)

Advancement of Surface Chemistry

Millions of people wear eyeglasses made with special nonreflecting glass. Mothers across the globe soothe their babies' diaper rash with ointments containing petroleum jelly. Students can study for 6,000 evening hours with the aid of a single, highly efficient light-bulb. Cooking and washing pots and pans have become relatively effortless processes since the invention of convenient cooking-oil sprays. All of the above are applications of technological advancements in the field of surface chemistry, a branch of science that deals with the chemical reactions that occur at the boundaries of two substances. Though this subfield of chemistry does not receive as much general attention as subfields such as biochemistry or organic chemistry, its uses permeate our everyday lives. In 1932, an industrial researcher named Irving Langmuir received the Nobel Prize in chemistry for his advancements in this field. His research career began with lightbulb chemistry but branched out to studies on atomic structure and atmospheric science. This amazing man had the gift of processing facts into theories that had an enormous range of practical applications.

Early Promise

Irving Langmuir was born in Brooklyn, New York, on January 31, 1881. He was the third of four sons of Charles and Sadie Comings Langmuir. As an executive for the New York Life Insurance Company, Charles was required to travel frequently. Irving attended public and private schools in both New York and Paris but did not enjoy the highly structured regimens. He was exceptionally bright and often knew more science than the schools offered, so school bored him. One instructor encouraged Irving to teach himself logarithms and trigonometry. In high school, he taught himself calculus in only six weeks. He also enjoyed conducting chemistry experiments, including making homemade bombs. His parents taught him to record daily detailed descriptions of observations, thoughts, and questions. Irving also enjoyed mountain climbing and attacked the Alps alone when he was only 12 years old. His father died in 1898, the same year that Irving graduated from Brooklyn's Pratt Institute High School. He subsequently enrolled at Columbia University.

Langmuir selected Columbia's School of Mines because it offered a more challenging combination of chemistry, physics, and mathematics than the other academic programs. In 1903, he earned a degree in metallurgical engineering. After graduation, he pursued postgraduate studies at the University of Göttingen, in Germany. His dissertation supervisor was the renowned physical chemist Walther Nernst, who in 1903 discovered the third law of thermodynamics, stating that entropy of a perfect crystal of an element approaches zero at a temperature of absolute zero. This work led to Nernst's receiving the 1920 Nobel Prize in chemistry. Nernst also developed a commercially successful electric lamp, with which Langmuir was involved. Langmuir's dissertation was titled "The Partial Recombination of Dissociated Gases during Cooling." In 1906, Langmuir also published another paper, "The Dissociation of Water Vapor and Carbon Dioxide at High Temperatures." In the future, he would pursue similar lines of investigation of chemical reactions occurring at high temperatures and low pressure.

Freedom to Pursue His Research

After obtaining both his master's and doctorate degrees in physical chemistry in 1906, Langmuir accepted a position as a chemistry instructor at the Stevens Institute of Technology (today the New Jersey Institute of Technology) in Hoboken, New Jersey. He enjoyed teaching very much, but the consuming demands of preparing lectures and laboratory lessons left him little time to conduct his own research on the velocity of reactions in gases moving through heated vessels. During the summer of 1909, he had the opportunity to work in the newly established Research Laboratory of the General Electric (G.E.) Company in Schenectady, New York. The lab was unique, as it was the first basic research laboratory situated in an industrial setting. The company gave academic freedom to its researchers, meaning scientists were permitted to pursue investigations that interested them even if they did not seem to be directly related to the company's goals. The director, Dr. Willis Whitney, excelled at recruiting geniuses to the lab and quickly recognized Langmuir's stifled creativity and brilliant mind. He encouraged Langmuir to work on whatever was fun rather than to worry about what could be practically applied, as most industrial research laboratories did.

Though Langmuir felt he did not accomplish anything for G.E., Whitney was anxious to have him permanently join his staff. Langmuir moved to Schenectady to join the full-time staff of G.E., where he remained for 40 years, eventually becoming associate director of the laboratory. His first assignment was to extend the life of lightbulbs, a project that was related to his graduate studies. At the time, ductile tungsten filaments enclosed in a vacuum were utilized in incandescent lamps (lamps in which an electrically heated filament emits light). A vacuum is a space from which the air has been removed. Since tungsten could be heated to extremely high temperatures, it glowed brilliantly and thus was an improvement over the formerly used, more delicate carbon filaments pioneered by Thomas Edison. However, the heated tungsten became weak and burned out, and the glass became blackened. When Langmuir measured the amount of gas produced by the lighted lamp, he discovered a quantity of gas equal to 7,000 times the volume of the filament. Further investigation revealed that the glass bulb released water vapor that reacted with the tungsten filament, giving off hydrogen. Langmuir also showed that in a vacuum, heating caused the tungsten atoms to evaporate from the wire when the temperature increased. The loss of atoms from the wire resulted in a thinner wire that broke easily. When he filled the tube with a gas that did not react with tungsten and switched to a coiled filament, it lasted longer. Filling the tubes with a mixture of nitrogen and argon gases increased the efficiency and lifetime of electric lamps. Langmuir received a patent for his improved incandescent bulb in 1916.

While conducting these studies, he also found that he could split molecules of hydrogen gas (H_2) into individual atoms of hydrogen by blowing hydrogen gas near hot tungsten. This discovery of atomic hydrogen eventually blossomed into the creation of a hydrogen welding torch that reached extremely hot temperatures from the energy released as the atoms of hydrogen recombined on the metal to be welded. He received a patent for this type of welding torch in 1934.

Because some scientists believed the blackening of bulbs was due to the inferior quality of the vacuum, studies on lightbulbs also led to more detailed research on vacuum pumps. In 1915, Langmuir invented a high-speed mercury-condensation vacuum pump that was 100 times more powerful than the existing pumps. This pump, combined with baked glass tubes, allowed the production of better-quality vacuum tubes. The new pump created vacuums approaching one-billionth of normal atmospheric pressure. The revolutionary high-vacuum tubes advanced technology in radio broadcasting, television, and cyclotron research.

In his personal life, Langmuir met Marion Mersereau, whom he married in 1912. She shared many of his interests such as skiing and music, and she supported his scientific endeavors. They later adopted a son and a daughter. He still enjoyed engaging in physical outdoor activities such as mountain climbing, skate-sailing, and hiking. After being encouraged by a neighbor, Langmuir started the first Boy Scout troop for teaching outdoor skills in Schenectady.

During World War I, the United States enlisted Langmuir's expertise to develop submarine detection devices using sonic waves. By employing two receivers, one could surmise the direction from which a sound originated. This research led to further work on stereophonic sound recording. After the war, he extended this research on sound recording in collaboration with the London-born American conductor Leopold Stokowski.

Refinement of the Atomic Structure Model

In 1916, American chemist Gilbert N. Lewis (1875–1946) proposed a mechanism for the formation of molecules. He defined a chemical bond as the sharing of a pair of electrons between two atoms. In this type of bond, known as a *covalent bond*, both participating atoms acquire a complete set of eight electrons in their outermost, or valence, shells in an effort to achieve stability. In *ionic bonds*, electrons are donated or accepted by individual atoms, rather than shared. A convenient method of notating the formation of bonds between atoms is named after Lewis. In *Lewis dot structures*, dots represent valence electrons which surround the nucleus, represented by the chemical symbol of

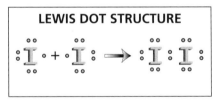

LEWIS DOT STRUCTURE

The Lewis dot structure is a convenient method for illustrating the role of electrons in covalent bond formation. In this example, two individual iodine atoms, each containing seven valence electrons, combine to form a molecule of iodine gas, in which each atom's valence shell has a complete octet of electrons.

the element. Lewis incorrectly believed that stationary electrons formed a cubical shape.

Langmuir examined the current theories on atomic structure during the period 1919–21 and extended Lewis's model for atomic structure to make it more significant to the scientific community. He modified the orbiting electron model proposed by the eminent Danish physicist Niels Bohr (1885–1962), who received the 1922 Nobel Prize in physics for his quantum mechanical model of the atom. Langmuir proposed that the electrons of atoms existed in concentric circles surrounding the nucleus and that all atoms were most stable with a complete set of eight electrons in their outer shell. The tendency of an atom to complete an octet in its outer shell determined its reactivity. For a while, chemists referred to the resulting octet theory of chemical valence as the Lewis-Langmuir electron dot theory, to which Lewis took offense. Langmuir presented a paper, "Arrangement of Electrons in Atoms and Molecules," to the American Physical Society in 1919. The members were so fascinated and impressed they asked Langmuir to read the 75-minute-long paper a second time.

Another field to which Langmuir made significant contributions was thermionic emissions. Thermionic emission is the flow of electrons from a metal during heating. From his studies on tungsten filaments, Langmuir found that the emission of electrons near tungsten's melting point was much lower than expected. He formulated what is known as the Child-Langmuir space-charge equation, which related the current between electrodes (conductors used to establish an electrical current) in a vacuum to voltage. (Clement Dexter Child [1868–1933] was a physicist at Colgate University in New York.) Space charge is the cloud of charged particles that maintains itself in the space between electrodes. Sometimes an unusually high thermionic emission was obtained, but no one knew why. Langmuir showed that this phenomenon was related to thorium oxide, which had been added to some of the filaments. He showed that the filament worked most efficiently when a layer of thoria only one molecule thick coated the filament. He next examined the phenomenon observed when cesium was added to a vacuum tube with a tungsten filament. If the tungsten filament was coated with a monatomic layer of oxygen, then cesium atoms were strongly adsorbed from the vapor onto the filament at a low temperature, resulting in very high thermionic emissions. Langmuir also found that the filament stole an electron from the cesium atom at higher temperatures, resulting in positively charged ions.

Langmuir examined the effect of electricity on gases and was among the first to study what he named "plasma," the unstable medium of gases charged with huge amounts of electricity. He also invented a special electrode for measuring electron temperature and ion density. His studies related to plasma led to advancements that had a major impact on later technology in astrophysics and atomic reactions.

Advancements in Surface Chemistry and the Nobel Prize

Though Langmuir had established himself in several fields of chemistry, his longest period of research was in the area of surface chemistry. Surface chemistry is the study of chemical forces and reactions that occur at the boundary between different substances.

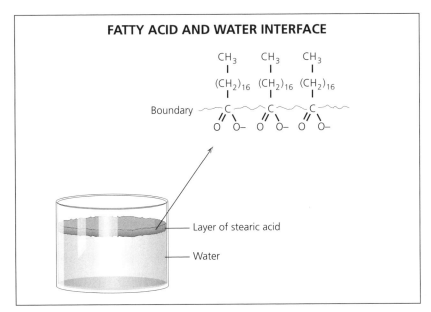

When a fatty acid such as stearic acid is layered over the surface of water, the hydrophobic hydrocarbon chains face upward and the hydrophilic carboxyl groups (COOH) protrude down into the water.

Katharine Burr Blodgett (1898–1979)

Katharine Burr Blodgett (1898–1979) was the first woman to become a General Electric Company scientist. She worked in the Schenectady laboratory under the supervision of Irving Langmuir. Langmuir-Blodgett technology is named after the two surface chemists. Her most famous creation, nonreflecting glass, is used throughout the world even today.

While working on a bachelor's degree at Bryn Mawr College, in Pennsylvania, Blodgett met Langmuir through some of her late father's former acquaintances who worked at G.E. Langmuir encouraged her to further her education. In 1918, she obtained a master's degree from the University of Chicago where she examined the adsorption of gases on charcoal, as used in gas masks. She soon joined G.E. as a research scientist and began collaborating with Langmuir. She started working on improving the tungsten filaments in electric lamps. After six years together, he encouraged her to earn her doctorate. She studied with Ernest Rutherford, who had earned a Nobel Prize in chemistry in 1908 for his

Langmuir saw a surface as a boundary between two substances rather than the top of something. He examined the behavior of oily films on aqueous surfaces. Because oil is not soluble in water, Langmuir predicted it would continue to spread out until it was only one molecule thick; at that point, he believed it would stop spreading due to adhesive forces between the molecules. Langmuir devised a method for measuring the spreading force of these films over liquids and for measuring the size of molecules by spreading layers of oil over water until a uniform thickness was obtained. Because saturated hydrocarbons (to be saturated is to contain the maximum possible number of hydrogen atoms) formed droplets rather than films over water, Langmuir deduced that the hydrocarbon chains of organic acids would upend the molecules on the investigations into the disintegration of the elements and the chemistry of radioactive substances. In 1926, Blodgett became the first woman to receive a doctorate degree in physics from the University of Cambridge.

She returned to G.E. and began working with Langmuir on monomolecular coatings, or films. In 1938, she successfully layered a 44-molecule-thick film onto a glass surface, creating nonreflecting, or invisible, glass. This type of glass is optimal for use in cameras and telescopes but is also used in eyeglasses and car windows. She obtained six U.S. patents relating to thin-film deposits, including one for a method of measuring film thickness based on the different colors that reflected off each successive layer. This field of research is referred to as Langmuir-Blodgett technology, one application of which deices airplane wings.

Later, she was involved in the work that led to smoke-screening methods used by the military and invented an instrument that was used in weather balloons to measure humidity in the upper atmosphere. Blodgett received several honorary doctorate degrees, as well as the Annual Achievement Award from the American Association of University Women in 1945 for her research in surface chemistry. In 1951, she became the first industrial research scientist to be awarded the Garvan Medal from the American Chemical Society.

water's surface. Organic acids, such as stearic acid, are long chains of carbon and hydrogen with a carboxyl group (COOH) attached to one end. Working with organic acids, he determined that at the interface, the *hydrophilic* polar groups (such as COOH) faced down into the aqueous substance and the *hydrophobic* regions (the hydrocarbon chains) faced upward. Langmuir also demonstrated that unsaturated hydrocarbon chains were more soluble in water due to the affinity of the double bonds for water.

Langmuir studied the process of *adsorption*, whereby molecules come into contact with and adhere to a surface without being absorbed. He found that gases often stuck to surfaces of liquids and solids in a single layer. Developing new methods, he studied the properties and kinetics of adsorbed species. Along with a dedicated collaborator, Katharine Blodgett, he pioneered a new approach to the field of surface chemistry by considering that chemical reactions occur in adsorbed films. Together, Langmuir and Blodgett studied monolayers, surface films only one atom or molecule thick that play an important role in biological processes. By dipping a sheet of metal through a film of stearic acid and withdrawing it again, they were able to form a monolayer on the surface of the metal with the molecules oriented so the acidic carboxyl groups (COOH) faced the metal and the hydrophobic chain faced outward. Each successive dip yielded two additional layers. The fatty acids were layered such that the hydrophobic ends always interacted with each other, as did the hydrophilic ends. Langmuir and Blodgett also worked out a method for layering films over glass. This led to the invention of nonreflecting, or almost perfectly transparent, glass.

In recognition of these discoveries and other investigations concerning surface chemistry, in 1932 Langmuir was awarded the Nobel Prize in chemistry. He was only the second American to receive a Nobel Prize in chemistry and the first industrial researcher to win one.

Controlling the Weather

During the Second World War, the military again sought Langmuir's expertise. He worked with an associate, Vincent Schaefer, and a colleague, Bernard Vonnegut, to create protective smoke screens. The beginning of this project was delayed, as Langmuir was diagnosed with cancer of the large intestine. He underwent two successful surgeries and completely recovered. The team performed light-scattering calculations to determine the optimal diameter of particle for blocking out light, so the movements of soldiers behind a white, smoky blanket would be undetectable by enemies. Then they built a smoke generator that was 100 times more powerful than the army's existing machines, and it was used all over Europe by the Allies. In addition, he worked on developing a gas-mask filter to remove smoky dust particles, and he researched deicing methods for aircrafts.

In the late 1930s, Langmuir changed his research focus to atmospheric science and meteorology, which he studied until his death. His interest in clouds grew from his love for mountain climbing and for flying airplanes, something he learned to do in 1930. His studies began in the laboratory, using a four-cubic-feet (113-dm³), black velvet-lined box. The inside temperature was kept subzero, and when he breathed into it the moisture condensed, forming a homemade cloud. One hot July, Schaefer was having trouble keeping the box cool enough to condense the water vapor, so he added a small chuck of dry ice (solid carbon dioxide) to the chamber. The box immediately filled with ice crystals. A similar effect was produced when any extremely cold material was added. Outdoor experiments commenced in 1946, when Schaefer brought six pounds (2.7 kg) of crushed dry ice onto a plane and scattered the granules over a supercooled cloud. Shortly afterward, the entire four-mile-long (6.4-m-long) cloud was converted into falling snow.

The team examined the formation of differently sized liquid particles in air and the formation of frozen precipitation. From 1940 to 1952, Langmuir served as the director of Project Cirrus, a joint program of the U.S. Army, Navy, and Air Force. He worked with Schaefer to devise methods for "seeding" clouds, using dry ice and silver iodide to create artificial rain and snow. The introduction of crystals into clouds formed the nucleus of a chain-reaction condensation. This method was not very practical, however, as it required flying over a cloud. On the suggestion of Vonnegut, they tried blowing fine particles of silver iodide, which have similar atomic dimensions to dry ice, upward from the ground. The results were even better than dropping dry-ice granules from above a cloud.

During the period 1949–52, Langmuir periodically seeded an area above New Mexico and then recorded the rainfall to the east. He also calculated the probability of rainfall and compared it to the observed rainfall following periodic seedings. He claimed that his weather modification experiments in New Mexico affected weather patterns in the Ohio Valley. Though the American Meteorological Society hesitated to accept his remarkable claims, this was the beginning of artificial weather control.

Langmuir officially retired in 1950 but continued to pursue his research and work as a consultant. In 1950, he published a book, *Phenomena, Atoms, and Molecules*, which was a collection of 20 of his most significant papers. Following a series of heart attacks, Langmuir died on August 16, 1957, in Falmouth, Massachusetts.

During his lifetime, Langmuir was awarded numerous medals including the American Chemical Society's Nichols Medal for his work on chemical reactions at low pressures (1915), the Royal Society's Hughes Medal for his research in molecular physics (1918), a second Nichols Medal for his work on atomic structure, the American Rumford Medal for his research on thermionic emissions and for his development of the gas-filled incandescent lamp (1920), the Cannizzaro Prize from the Royal Academy of Lincei at Rome (1925), the Perkin Medal from the American Society of Chemical Industry (1928), the Chandler Medal from Columbia University (1930), the American Chemical Society's Willard Gibbs Medal (1930), the *Popular Science Monthly* annual medal (1932), the Franklin Medal of the Franklin Institute (1934), the Holly Medal of the American Society of Mechanical Engineers (1934), the Faraday Medal from the Chemical Society of London (1938), the Faraday Medal from the British Institute of Electrical Engineers (1944), and the Mascart Medal from the French Society of Electricians (1950). Langmuir was honored with 15 doctorates. He was a member of the National Academy of Sciences and a fellow of the American Physical Society, and he was a foreign member of the Royal Society of London and the Chemical Society of London. Langmuir served as president of the American Chemical Society in 1929 and president of the American Association for the Advancement of Science in 1941. He published more than 200 scientific articles during the course of his career and was issued 63 patents.

Langmuir's abounding mental energy led to many discoveries in a variety of chemistry subfields. He made significant contributions to at least seven different areas of scientific research: chemical reactions at high temperatures and low pressures, thermal effects in gases, atomic structure, thermionic emission and surfaces in vacuum, chemical forces in solids, liquids, and surface films, electrical discharges in gases, and atmospheric science. His invention of high-vacuum electron tubes revolutionized electrical technology, and his invention of the gas-filled incandescent lamp has saved millions of dollars' worth of electricity for consumers. Langmuir was an enthusiastic researcher, but he also was a well-rounded person who enjoyed physical outdoor activities and spending time with his children. He took pleasure in sharing his knowledge with them as well as with the rest of the world.

CHRONOLOGY

1881	Irving Langmuir is born in Brooklyn, New York, on January 31
1903	Earns a degree in metallurgical engineering from Columbia University
1906	Receives a master's and a doctorate in physical chemistry from the University of Göttingen, Germany.
1906–09	Teaches at the Stevens Institute of Technology in Hoboken, New Jersey
1909	Joins the G.E. Research Laboratory in Schenectady, New York. He works there for 40 years, eventually becoming associate director. Begins research to improve lightbulbs
1915	Invents high-speed mercury-condensation vacuum pump
1917	Works on submarine detection research for the U.S. government
1919	Presents the paper "Arrangement of Electrons in Atoms and Molecules" to the American Physical Society
1932	Becomes the first American industrial chemist to receive the Nobel Prize in chemistry, awarded for his discoveries and investigations in surface chemistry
1946	Begins experiments seeding supercooled clouds to make artificial rain and snow
1950	Publishes compilation of his research, *Phenomena, Atoms, and Molecules*. Officially retires from G.E., but keeps his office and continues to consult
1957	Dies on August 16, following a series of heart attacks in Falmouth, Massachusetts

FURTHER READING

Asimov, Isaac. *Breakthroughs in Science.* Boston, Mass.: Houghton Mifflin, 1959. Well-written, entertaining reference book about 26 scientific discoveries. Intended for middle and high school students.

Biographical Memoirs. National Academy of Sciences. Vol. 45. Washington, D.C.: National Academy of Sciences, 1974. Memoir of Langmuir's life and accomplishments written by two distinguished colleagues.

Garraty, John A., and Mark C. Carnes, eds. *American National Biography.* Vol. 13. New York: Oxford University Press, 1999. Brief account of lives and works of famous Americans in encyclopedia format.

Gillispie, Charles C., ed. *Dictionary of Scientific Biography.* Vol. 8. New York: Scribner, 1970–76. Good source for facts concerning personal background and scientific accomplishments but assumes basic knowledge of science.

Nobelprize.org. "The Nobel Prize in Chemistry 1932." Available online. URL: http://nobelprize.org/chemistry/laureates/1932/. Last modified June 16, 2000. Includes links to Langmuir's Nobel lecture, banquet speech, biography, and other resources.

Thompson, Kathleen, and Alice Veyvoda. "Irving Langmuir." Woodrow Wilson Leadership Program in Chemistry. Available online. URL:http://www.woodrow.org/teachers/chemistry/institutes/1992/Langmuir.html. Accessed February 3, 2005. Easily readable biography of Langmuir, including a useful bibliography.

Westervelt, Virginia. *Incredible Man of Science.* New York: Julian Messner, 1968. Biography of Langmuir's life and important contributions to scientific knowledge. Complicated science is clearly explained through imagined conversations between Langmuir and his family.

Emil Hermann Fischer

6

(1852–1919)

Emil Fischer made several significant advances in organic chemistry while studying hydrazine derivatives, purines, sugars, amino acids, proteins, and enzymes. (© *The Nobel Foundation*)

Synthesis of Purines and Sugars and the Mechanism of Enzyme Action

If two children were each provided with a box of sticks and differently shaped blocks, they could build a number of potential structures. Even if they used the same number of sticks and same-shaped blocks, the different possibilities are numerous. Though gloves all have a palm side, a back side, four protrusions for fingers, and one for a thumb, the difference between one that fits on the right hand

and one that fits on the left becomes quite apparent when trying to put on the gloves. Structural details matter in these two illustrations and also in organic chemistry.

A German chemist named Emil Fischer was one of the most versatile organic chemists of all time. He studied organic dyes, discovered *phenylhydrazine*, characterized and synthesized caffeine and related compounds, and studied sugars and *purines*. He was the first to emphasize the importance of not only position but orientation of atoms within a molecule. Already considered an ingenious organic chemist, his work on *amino acids* and *enzymes* made him a founder of peptide chemistry and a pioneer of biochemistry.

A Choice of Science

Emil Hermann Fischer was born on October 9, 1852, to Laurenz and Julie Poensgen Fischer in Euskirchen, Germany (near Bonn).

Kekulé and Benzene

German chemist Friedrich August Kekulé (1829–96) was a professor at the University of Bonn from 1867 to 1896. In the mid-19th century, chemists doubted that the structures of molecules could be determined accurately since they would be disrupted during analysis. Though Kekulé was not a brilliant experimentalist, while riding on a bus he experienced a daydream that gave him insight into the structure of molecules. He pictured the atoms assembling themselves into defined arrangements in space. This event stimulated the formation of his molecular structural theory, which he proposed in an 1858 paper titled "On the Constitution and Metamorphoses of Chemical Compounds and the Chemical Nature of Carbon." He stated that carbon atoms may combine with one another to form long chains and that carbon was tetravalent, meaning that

He was their first son, though their sixth child. Emil began his schooling with a private tutor, then attended local schools at Euskirchen, Wetzlar, and Bonn and graduated in 1869 at the top of his class. His father was a lumber merchant who had dreams of his son entering the family business. Emil proved to be a failure in business, however, so in 1871, his father allowed him to pursue physics at the University of Bonn, where he attended lectures given by the German chemist Friedrich August Kekulé. Emil's cousin, Otto Fischer, convinced him to transfer to the recently established University of Strasbourg the following year. Under the influence of Adolf von Baeyer, Emil obtained his degree in chemistry.

A Chemist on the Move

Fischer received a doctorate degree in chemistry in 1874 from the University of Strasbourg with a dissertation on the phthalein dyes

it would form a total of four chemical bonds when combining with other atoms. Together, these ideas form the foundation of structural organic chemistry. Kekulé also believed that one could glean information about the structure of the reactants of a chemical reaction from the structure of the products, a concept utilized by Emil Fischer in unraveling the structures of many different types of organic molecules.

Kekulé is most recognized for his discovery of the structure of *benzene* in 1865. Benzene is the most common member of a family named the aromatic hydrocarbons, all the members of which have stable, ringed structures that contain alternating single and double bonds. Chemists knew that benzene had a molecular formula of C_6H_6 but were baffled as to how the atoms were arranged to meet valence requirements. Once again, the answer came to Kekulé in a dream, this time during a nap in front of the fireplace. He determined that the carbon atoms formed a ring with alternating single and double bonds. One hydrogen atom also was bonded to each carbon, so the total number of bonds in which each carbon atom participated was four.

fluorescein and orcin-phthalein. He obtained an assistant instructorship under Baeyer at Strasbourg and followed him to the University of Munich in 1875. He became a *Privatdozent* (unpaid lecturer) in organic chemistry in 1878, then, in 1879, an assistant professor of analytical chemistry. He moved again in 1881, when the University of Erlangen appointed him professor of chemistry. In 1888, Fischer was appointed professor of chemistry at the University of Würzburg, and then, in 1892, he moved to the University of Berlin to serve as the chairman of the chemistry department. He remained in Berlin until his death. His research covered a broad range of topics and the dates of his studies overlapped somewhat, thus it is best to review his work by subject rather than chronologically.

Fischer married Agnes Gerlach in 1888, but she died after only seven years of marriage. They had three sons together. One tragically was killed in World War I and another committed suicide, but the third, Hermann Otto Laurenz Fischer, became a renowned professor of biochemistry at the University of California at Berkeley.

An Early Discovery

At Strasbourg, Fischer began studying hydrazine derivatives, that is, molecules made from hydrazine, which he named. Hydrazine (NH_2NH_2) is an inorganic compound of two nitrogen atoms linked to each other and to two hydrogen atoms each. Fischer's former professor from Bonn, Kekulé, previously had proposed a formula for diazonium compounds (a type of compound with two nitrogen atoms joined by a double bond) that several chemists did not believe was true. Fischer performed experiments verifying Kekulé's formula, then went on to discover phenylhydrazine ($C_6H_5NHNH_2$). Phenylhydrazine was the first hydrazine base; it is used in the synthesis of pesticides, pharmaceuticals, and dyes, and its discovery led to the development by others of synthetic drugs such as novacaine. The Fischer phenylhydrazine synthesis is named after him. Fischer explored the possible industrial applications of phenylhydrazine derivatives and later depended on this compound to purify sugars and distinguish between sugar isomers. (Isomers are compounds that have the same molecular formula but different structures.)

At Munich, Fischer and his cousin Otto examined the constitution of dyes derived from triphenylmethane. Together, they determined the constitution of rosaniline and pararosaniline as being triamine derivatives (meaning three amine groups have been added) of triphenylmethane and its homologues.

What Caffeine and Barbituates Have in Common

At Erlangen, Fischer began studying uric acid and stimulants found within tea and coffee, mainly caffeine and theobromine. This evolved into three decades of research on the structures of molecules which, like uric acid and caffeine, all contained a molecular group with the formula $C_5N_4H_4$ that Fischer named a "purine." Purines are molecules that are similar in that they are composed of a bicyclic (two-ringed) nitrogenous structure but differ by the addition of different side groups, such as hydroxyl or amino groups. Fischer synthesized this heterocyclic structure in 1898. The most talked about purine bases are adenine and guanine, which are components of nucleotides, the building blocks of nucleic acids such as deoxyribonucleic acid, or DNA. Using the principle proposed by Kekulé that said structural clues about molecules could be uncovered from information about their reaction products, Fischer performed numerous chemical analyses and degradations on purines and studied the products. He studied purines from 1881 to 1914, when he became the first to successfully synthesize a nucleotide, theophylline-d-glucoside phosphoric acid. Theophylline is used to treat chronic asthma by relaxing the smooth muscles which contract the airways. Fischer synthesized a total of more than 130 purines.

Industries adopted the methods Fischer developed while studying purines to synthesize caffeine, theophylline, and theobromine. Industry also took notice when Fischer started synthesizing other purines called barbiturates, depressant drugs which act on the central nervous system. In 1903, he synthesized 5,5-diethyl-barbituric acid, also known as barbital, which is used as a sedative and a hypnotic

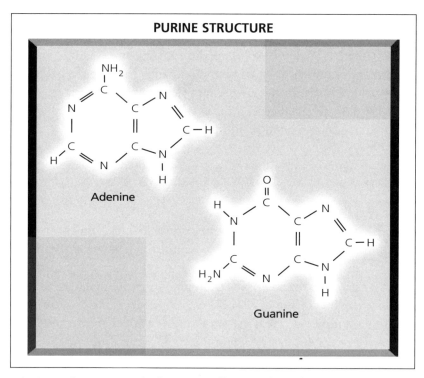

Adenine and guanine are both purines. All purines have the heterocyclic carbon-nitrogen ringed structure.

drug. In 1912, Fischer synthesized phenobarbital, also a depressant, which is used as a sedative or hypnotic as well as an anticonvulsant in lower doses.

Differences in Sugars

Among Fischer's most important accomplishments were the structural characterization and then synthesis of the sugars *glucose*, *fructose*, and *mannose* from *glycerol*. The most common sugars contain six carbon atoms, each linked to an oxygen atom, with as many hydrogen atoms as necessary to meet valence requirements. The structural differences between the sugars that he studied were minute but extremely important biologically. Phenylhydrazine, which he previously had discovered, was instrumental in distinguishing between forms. He performed a series of exhaustive tests on the stereochemical nature, or three-dimensional arrangement, of atoms that make up sugar molecules and figured out that some sugars, such as glucose and mannose, only differed in the orientation of a single asymmetric carbon in the molecule. He also predicted all the possible stereoisomers of glucose. Stereoisomers are molecules that have the same bonding order of atoms but differ in the way the atoms are arranged in space. *Enantiomers* are one type of stereoisomer in which the molecules are mirror images of one another. Diastereomers are stereoisomers that are not mirror images. Glucose and mannose are diastereomers because they have opposite configurations at the second carbon atom, but they are not mirror images of one another. In fact, they are *epimers*, sugars that differ in configuration at only a single asymmetric center.

In 1902, Fischer was awarded the Nobel Prize in chemistry for his research on sugar and purine syntheses. By this time, he had already begun to systematically study *proteins* in the same manner

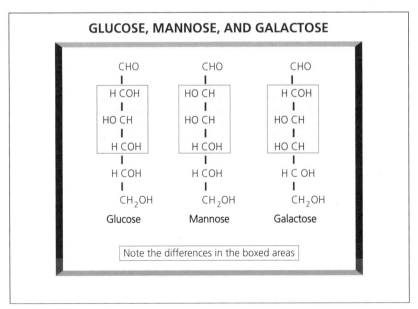

GLUCOSE, MANNOSE, AND GALACTOSE

Note the differences in the boxed areas

The sugars glucose, mannose, and galactose are distinct yet very similar in structure. Because they differ only in their configuration around a single carbon atom, glucose and mannose are considered epimers, as are glucose and galactose. All three are diastereomers.

as he investigated sugars and purines. He later received the Helmholtz Medal (1909) from the Royal Academy of Sciences of Berlin for his work on sugars as well as his research on protein chemistry.

Amino Acids and Proteins

Between 1899 and 1908, Fischer switched his focus to proteins. While attempting to purify and identify individual amino acids, he adapted a technique for separating amino acids that was originally developed by Theodor Curtius in 1883. Fischer prepared esters of the amino acids and then separated them by distillation. Using this methodology he discovered the amino acid valine and the cyclic

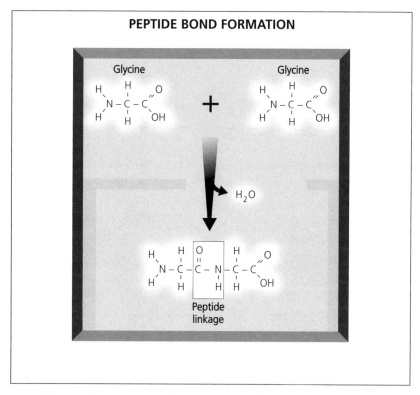

A peptide bond is formed when the carbon atom from the carboxyl group of one amino acid covalently binds to the nitrogen atom from a second amino acid, releasing a molecule of water.

amino acids proline and hydroxyproline. In 1901 and 1902, he synthesized the amino acids ornithine and serine, respectively. He synthesized a third, cysteine, in 1908.

Fischer researched the synthesis of proteins and defined a *peptide bond* as the amide linkage between two amino acids. Using optically pure amino acids, he was able to link two glycines, forming the dipeptide glycyl-glycine. By attacking either the amino or the carbonyl group of the amino acid, he was able to synthesize linked chains of several amino acids, eventually synthesizing a chain of 15 glycine and three leucine amino acids. This synthetic *polypeptide* and others that he synthesized showed many characteristics similar to proteins. Because of these accomplishments, Fischer is considered a founder of peptide chemistry.

Lock and Key

Enzymes are biological catalysts, that is, they speed up the rate of a chemical reaction more than one millionfold without being consumed in the process. Enzymes function by bringing the reactive parts of molecules close to one another to facilitate the natural chemical reaction. They work in a very specific manner, only catalyzing their own particular reaction and no others. An enzyme recognizes *substrate* molecules by their precise shape and can distinguish between molecules that differ by only a single stereometric configuration.

Using yeast, a single-celled organism from the kingdom Fungi, Fischer studied the enzymatic reactions occurring during sugar fermentation. Fermentation is the process whereby sugars and other organic molecules are broken down without using oxygen. Some of their stored energy is released during breakdown for use by the organism. Fischer determined that enzymes are uniquely designed, asymmetric molecules and proposed the lock-and-key model for enzyme action in 1894. Just as a key only fits into and works on a particular lock, enzymes only bind to and act on specific substrates, molecules that participate in the chemical reaction the enzyme catalyzes. Thus, the enzyme that catalyzes a chemical transformation in the fermentation of glucose would not also recognize, say, mannose.

The Death of a Remarkable Organic Chemist

Before World War I, Fischer had begun to study tannins, a type of acid extracted from vegetables. During the war, he helped organize chemical inventory and resources and coordinated the production of chemicals used in the production of explosives and foods. His work led to the invention of a butter substitute, ester margarine.

In 1919, Fischer died in Berlin. Some sources claim the cause of death was cancer, while other reports claim suicide. The German Chemical Society instituted the Emil Fischer Memorial Medal in his honor. During his lifetime, Fischer had been made a Prussian *Geheimrat* (excellency) and was awarded honorary doctorates from the Universities of Christiania, Cambridge, Manchester, and Brussels. Though he was a pure researcher, many of his discoveries had direct industrial applications, such as the bulk production of caffeine, sugars, and pharmaceuticals. His numerous notable achievements stimulated astounding growth in the field of organic chemistry, and his research on sugars, purines, proteins, and enzymes laid the foundations for the field of biochemistry, the study of the molecular basis of life. Not only was Fischer responsible for determining the structures of many organic molecules, including purines, sugars, and amino acids, he was also the first to synthesize many of them. A master of organic synthesis and analysis, Fischer clearly deserved his 1902 Nobel Prize in chemistry.

CHRONOLOGY

1852	Emil Hermann Fischer is born on October 9 at Euskirchen, Germany
1871	Enters the University of Bonn to study chemistry
1872	Enrolls at the University of Strasbourg
1874	Researches phthalein dyes and obtains doctorate in chemistry from the University of Strasbourg
1878	Becomes a privatdozent in organic chemistry at the University of Munich

1879	Is appointed assistant professor of analytical chemistry at the University of Munich
1881	Becomes a professor of chemistry at the University of Erlangen and begins studying purines
1882–06	Studies purines and sugars
1888	Is appointed professor of chemistry at the University of Würzburg
1892	Becomes chairman of chemistry at the University of Berlin
1894	Proposes lock-and-key model for enzyme action
1898	Synthesizes the first of 130 purines
1899–08	Studies amino acids and proteins and defines a peptide bond
1902	Receives the Nobel Prize in chemistry in recognition of the extraordinary services he renders by his work on sugar and purine syntheses
1903	Synthesizes the sedative barbital
1914	Becomes the first chemist to synthesize a nucleotide
1919	Dies in Berlin on July 15. The German Chemical Society institutes the Emil Fischer Memorial Medal

FURTHER READING

Farber, Eduard. *Nobel Prize Winners in Chemistry 1901–1961.* New York: Abelard-Schuman, 1963. Profiles 66 chemists who won the Nobel Prize in chemistry, with brief biological sketches, short descriptions of the prize-winning work, and explanations of the significance of their research.

Gillispie, Charles C., ed. *Dictionary of Scientific Biography.* Vol. 5. New York: Scribner, 1970–76. Good source for facts concerning personal background and scientific accomplishments but assumes basic knowledge of science.

Nobelprize.org. "The Nobel Prize in Chemistry 1902." Available online. URL: http://nobelprize.org/chemistry/laureates/1902/.

Last modified June 16, 2000. Includes links to Fischer's biography and Nobel lecture.

Simmons, John. *The Scientific 100: A Ranking of the Most Influential Scientists, Past and Present*. Secaucus, N.J.: Carol Publishing Group, 1996. Rankings of 100 broadly ranging scientists with justification describing their achievements.

7

Gerty Cori

(1896–1957)

Gerty Cori performed pioneering research on carbohydrate biochemistry and the enzymes that operate metabolic pathways. (© The Nobel Foundation)

Sugar Metabolism and Glycogen Storage Disorders

Carbohydrates are the body's major source of energy for performing any work, such as contracting muscles to grip a pencil or duplicating genetic material preceding cell division. Energy that is taken into the body in the form of food is chemically broken down into simpler substances that can be absorbed into blood circulation and transported to all body tissues. In the digestive tract, enzymes digest the ingested carbohydrates first into *disaccharides* (such as lactose and sucrose) and then into *monosaccharides* (such as fructose or glucose). Glucose is a simple sugar consisting of six carbon atoms, and it is stored in animal cells in the form of *glycogen*, a natural polymer made of branches of chains of linked glucose molecules. When the body tissues need energy, glucose molecules can be removed from glycogen.

Biochemists study the chemical processes that occur in living organisms. Gerty Cori was a pioneer biochemist whose research focused on how the body uses and stores sugars. In collaboration with her husband, Carl Cori, she elucidated the pathways of metabolic intermediates between glycogen and glucose and identified and characterized many of the enzymes involved. Later in her career she studied childhood disorders of carbohydrate *metabolism* and related deficiencies of particular enzymes to specific inherited disorders.

A Life Partnership

Gerty Theresa Radnitz was the oldest of three daughters born to Otto and Martha Radnitz on August 15, 1896, in Prague, Austria-Hungary (now part of the Czech Republic). Her father was a chemist and a general manager of a beet-sugar refinery. His career and the fact that he suffered from diabetes may have influenced Gerty's choice of research topics later in life. Gerty was educated by a private tutor until the age of 10, when she entered a school for girls to learn culture and social etiquette. Though she was bright, females were not afforded the same educational opportunities as males at the time. Universities officially enrolled female students, but in actuality very few were admitted. Gerty's preparatory education had not exposed her to the prerequisite Latin, mathematics, and science courses necessary for acceptance. An uncle who was a professor of pediatrics recognized her intellect and encouraged her to pursue an advanced education. During a family vacation when she was 16, she met a high school teacher who taught her three years of Latin over the course of one summer. Within two years, Gerty had mastered all the subjects necessary to pass the university entrance examination. She entered Carl Ferdinand University, the German University of Prague, in 1914, with plans to study medicine, the common pathway to her desired career in biomedical research.

During her first year, she met a fellow student named Carl Cori in her anatomy class. They collaborated on a research project examining *complement*, a component of the immune system. They climbed mountains and skied together during vacations and fell in love. In 1920, they graduated, moved to Vienna, and married. Carl obtained a job at the University Pharmacological Institute, and Gerty worked as an assistant at the Karolinen Children's Hospital. She studied the role of the thyroid gland in regulation of body temperature. When Carl moved to the University of Graz, Gerty stayed in Vienna. Conditions were devastating in postwar Europe, and she developed xerophthalmia (a disease caused by a lack of vitamin A in which the eyes become dry and susceptible to infections) from malnutrition. She recovered with a better diet after briefly returning to her parents' home in Prague. Though Gerty converted to Catholicism before marrying Carl, it became obvious that her Jewish heritage would prevent Carl from advancement in his career in Europe, so they began looking for positions in America.

Carl Cori accepted a job at the New York State Institute for the Study of Malignant Diseases (now called the Roswell Park Cancer Institute) in Buffalo. Six months later, Gerty Cori followed and took a job as an assistant pathologist, with duties well below her capabilities and training. Though she had the same scientific background as her husband, Cori had the disadvantage of being a woman. She battled this gender discrimination for the majority of her career. Carl was strongly advised against collaborating with his wife, and she was warned to stay out of his lab. Despite this, they collaborated on numerous projects for almost four decades, and it is sometimes difficult to distinguish which Cori performed what research. Gerty researched the effects of X-rays on the skin and organs during her first few years in Buffalo, but together they developed an interest in carbohydrate metabolism, beginning their decades-long collaboration on this subject.

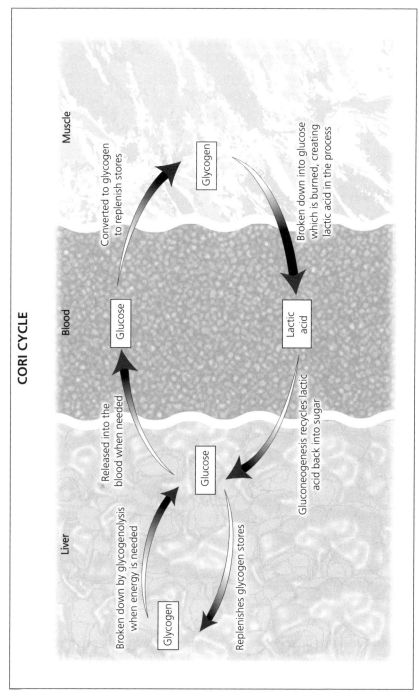

The Coris proposed a cycle that linked glucose with glycogen and lactic acid.

by determining in laboratory animals the percentage of ingested glucose that was converted to fat and the percentage that was stored as glycogen. These studies required great precision and accuracy with measurements, a quality that was characteristic of the Coris' work.

Fully absorbed in the mysteries of carbohydrate metabolism, Gerty delved into a series of studies examining the rates of absorption of sugars from the small intestine and measuring the levels of products of carbohydrate metabolism such as glycogen and lactic acid. She realized that an intermediate between muscle and liver glycogen must exist, since muscle glycogen did not increase blood glucose levels, whereas liver glycogen did. After six years of research, in 1929 Cori and her husband proposed the cycle of carbohydrates, called the Cori cycle by others. (These studies spanned their work in Buffalo and St. Louis.)

In a series of papers, the Coris described the roles of certain *hormones* on the regulation of carbohydrate metabolism. In 1921, the effect of the hormone *insulin* on blood sugar levels had been discovered by Frederick Banting and Charles Best at the University of Toronto. In one form of untreated diabetes, blood sugar levels become elevated due to the patient's inability to produce enough insulin, which is necessary to transport glucose into the body's cells. Banting and Best found that injections of insulin brought blood glucose levels back down to normal levels.

The Coris decided to explore the effect of insulin and another hormone, *epinephrine*, on glucose metabolism. Also called adrenalin, epinephrine is a hormone secreted by the adrenal glands in times of high stress. They found that insulin treatment increased the amount of glucose converted to muscle glycogen but decreased the conversion to liver glycogen. The administration of epinephrine, on the other hand, had the opposite effect. In addition to increasing the heart rate and blood pressure, epinephrine increased the amount of available glucose for extra energy. They also observed an increase in the conversion of muscle glycogen to lactate and the formation of a hexose monophosphate (a six-carbon sugar with a phosphate group attached). In 1936, they identified the hexose monophosphate as glucose-1-phosphate.

Chemistry in a Test Tube

In 1928, Cori and her husband became naturalized citizens of the United States. While initially they had been interested in studying the excess stored glucose and the high formation of lactic acid from glucose in tumors, they could no longer justify performing their pure carbohydrate biochemistry research in a center dedicated to studying malignant tumors. Though they had published 50 scientific papers together while at the Institute for the Study of Malignant Diseases, Gerty was treated unfairly and was told her presence was hindering her husband's career. In 1931, the Coris moved to St. Louis, Missouri, where they both accepted positions at the Washington University School of Medicine. Carl was made a professor of pharmacology, and in 1942, he became a professor of biochemistry. Gerty was given the untenured position of research associate in the department of pharmacology. The rampant gender discrimination common at the time prevented her from a more deserved title, but at least they were able to continue their collaborative research on carbohydrate metabolism. They progressed from animal studies to in vitro investigations.

Chemists believed that glycogen was broken down into individual glucose molecules by *hydrolysis*, the simple chemical breakdown of a chain of molecules by the addition of water. Gerty Cori showed this was incorrect; the process was much more complicated. In 1936, she discovered and isolated from minced frog muscle an intermediate in the breakdown of glycogen to glucose, the compound glucose-1-phosphate, referred to as the Cori ester, a glucose molecule with one phosphate group attached to the first carbon atom. Fellow chemists were amazed in 1939, when the Coris utilized their knowledge and purified enzymes to synthesize glycogen in vitro, the first biochemical synthesis of a large molecule done in a test tube. Cori showed that the enzyme phosphorylase tears apart the bonds that link the hundreds of glucose molecules to form glycogen. Phosphorylase also catalyzes the reverse reaction of glucose-1-phosphate with glycogen, adding a glucose molecule to the glycogen chain and releasing free phosphate. After being purified from muscle tissue, phosphorylase was crystallized and characterized in 1942 and 1943, respectively, followed by the identification and isolation of several other enzymes involved in glycogen metabolism.

In 1938, the Coris found another intermediate in carbohydrate metabolism, glucose-6-phosphate, a glucose molecule with a phosphate group attached to the sixth carbon atom. This compound could be formed either by the conversion of glucose-1-phosphate by the enzyme now called phosphoglucomutase, which they discovered, or by the *phosphorylation* (addition of a phosphate group by the enzyme hexokinase) of glucose using adenosine triphosphate (ATP). They then elucidated the metabolic pathway leading from glucose-6-phosphate to glycogen.

During all this excitement at work, the Coris welcomed the arrival of their only son, Carl Thomas ("Tom") Cori, in 1936. To the parents' dismay, Tom was not interested in following their footsteps into academic research. He earned a doctorate degree in chemistry but went on to become president of one of the most reputable chemical production companies, Sigma-Aldrich.

First American Female Nobel Prize Recipient

By the 1940s, the Coris had outlined a fairly complete map of carbohydrate metabolism. Washington University finally promoted Gerty Cori to the position of associate professor with tenure at Washington University in 1944; her husband was promoted to a full professor of biochemistry. Other universities including Harvard and the Rockefeller Institute competed for the Coris in their own departments, but in 1946 Washington University offered Carl the chairmanship of a new biochemistry department, convincing them to remain in St. Louis. In 1947, Carl granted Gerty a full professorship. That same year, Gerty fainted while climbing the Rocky Mountains with her husband. She was diagnosed with *agnogenic myeloid dysplasia*, a fatal type of anemia that eventually would claim her life.

In October of 1947, the Coris shared the Nobel Prize in physiology or medicine for their discovery of the course of the catalytic conversion of glycogen. Cori was only the third woman to be awarded a Nobel Prize in science (the other two were Marie Curie and Irène Joliot-Curie), but she was the first American woman to be awarded the honor. The Argentinian physiologist Bernardo A. Houssay won the other half for his discovery of the part played by the hormone of the anterior pituitary lobe in the metabolism of sugar. Carl and Gerty both presented portions of the Nobel lecture in Stockholm.

Glycogen Storage Diseases

Despite her failing health, Cori continued her research efforts full throttle. She set up an army cot in her office to rest when she became overtired, and her husband monitored her *hemoglobin* levels and blood transfusions. She switched her research focus to childhood inherited glycogen metabolic disorders.

GLYCOGEN

Individual glucose residues

Branch point

Glycogen is a highly branched polymer made of hundreds of glucose molecules linked together and used to store energy in animal cells.

In the early 1950s, Gerty Cori determined the exact structure of the highly branched glycogen molecule by chemically degrading it, step by step, using the enzymes she had identified and purified throughout the years. This discovery enabled her to identify two specific diseases of carbohydrate metabolism: one where the glycogen structure was abnormal and one where too much glycogen was stored. Both disorders resulted from deficiencies of enzymes involved in glycogen metabolic pathways. Her finding was a breakthrough in the study of metabolic disorders, as she was the first to demonstrate that an enzyme deficiency can cause a specific disease. She identified two additional enzymatic defects linked to metabolic diseases; medical researchers have identified at least six more since then.

Death of a Hero

Cori published her last scientific paper, "Biochemical Aspects of Glycogen Deposition Disease," in *Modern Problems in Pediatrics*, in 1957. She passed away at home with her husband at her side at age 61, on October 26, 1957. During her lifetime, she had been a member of the American Society of Biological Chemists, the National Academy of Sciences, and the American Chemical Society (ACS). President Harry Truman appointed her to the board of the National Science Foundation, where she contributed to the establishment of guidelines for governmental support of scientific research. With her husband, she had been awarded the Midwest Award from the ACS (1946) and the Squibb Award in Endocrinology (1947). Independently, she was awarded the Garvan Medal (1948), the St. Louis Award (1948), the Sugar Research Prize (1950), the Borden Award (1951), and several honorary doctorate degrees. In addition to the Coris themselves, six scholars trained in the Coris' laboratories became Nobel laureates: Severo Ochoa and Arthur Kornberg (physiology or medicine 1959), Luis F. Leloir (chemistry 1970), Earl W. Sutherland (physiology or medicine 1971), Christian R. de Duve (physiology or medicine 1974), and Edwin G. Krebs (physiology or medicine 1992).

Kind and passionate but tough, Gerty Cori demanded perfection from herself and her colleagues and maintained a strong commitment to intellectual integrity. These qualities enabled her to decipher the body's mechanisms for regulating the balance between glucose in the blood and stored glycogen in the liver and muscles. Her careful methodology and creative genius led her through the characterization of several enzymes involved in carbohydrate metabolism. Her research had direct clinical applications, as she demonstrated that deficiencies or defects in the function of specific enzymes caused a group of diseases termed glycogen storage disorders.

CHRONOLOGY

1896	Gerty Radnitz is born on August 15 in Prague, part of the Austro-Hungarian Empire (now Czech Republic)
1914	Passes the university entrance examination at the Tetschen Realgymnasium and enters the German University of Prague
1920	Receives doctorate in medicine from the medical school of the German University of Prague
1920–22	Works at the Karolinen Children's Hospital in Vienna
1922	Joins husband Carl Cori as an assistant pathologist at the Institute for the Study of Malignant Disease in Buffalo, New York, and develops an interest in carbohydrate metabolism
1929	Proposes Cori cycle with husband
1931	Accepts position as research associate in pharmacology at Washington University in St. Louis, Missouri
1936	Discovers and isolates glucose-1-phosphate, an intermediate in the breakdown of glycogen to glucose
1939	Synthesizes glycogen in vitro in collaboration with husband
1944	Is promoted to associate professor with tenure at Washington University

1947	Gerty and Carl Cori receive the Nobel Prize in physiology or medicine for their discovery of the course of the catalytic conversion of glycogen. They share the prize with Bernardo Alberto Houssay for his discovery of the part played by the hormone of the anterior pituitary lobe in the metabolism of sugar. Gerty Cori is promoted to full professor of biochemistry
1951	Switches focus of research to enzymatic defects of glycogen metabolism and storage
1957	Dies on October 26 following a lengthy illness at age 61

FURTHER READING

Biographical Memoirs. National Academy of Sciences. Vol. 61. Washington, D.C.: National Academy of Sciences, 1992. Memoirs of Gerty Cori's and Carl Cori's lives and accomplishments written by distinguished colleagues.

Garraty, John A., and Mark C. Carnes, eds. *American National Biography.* Vol. 5. New York: Oxford University Press, 1999. Brief accounts of the lives and works of famous Americans in encyclopedia format.

McGrayne, Sharon Bertsch. *Nobel Prize Women in Science.* Washington, D.C.: Joseph Henry Press, 1998. Examines the lives and achievements of 15 women who either won a Nobel Prize or played a crucial role in a Nobel Prize–winning project.

Nobelprize.org. "The Nobel Prize in Physiology or Medicine 1947." Available online. URL: http://nobelprize.org/medicine/ laureates/1947/. Last modified June 16, 2000. Includes links to Gerty Cori's biography and Nobel lecture as well as those of Carl Cori and Bernardo Alberto Houssay.

Roberts, Russell. *American Women of Medicine.* Berkeley Heights, N.J.: Enslow Publishers, 2002. Examines the lives of 10 women who overcame obstacles to pursue careers in medicine.

Percy Julian

8

(1899–1975)

Percy Julian developed methods for synthesizing products from substances extracted from soybean. *(DePauw University Archives and Special Collections)*

Synthesis of Glaucoma Drug and Sterols from Natural Plant Products

Developing countries depend on traditional medicine to treat a variety of maladies. For example, ginger is used to relieve nausea, stimulate circulation, and fight headaches, and eucalyptus is used as an antiseptic and to relieve coughing. The active ingredients of one-fourth of all drugs prescribed in the United States are either derived from or extracted from plants. For example, the painkiller morphine

interested in the chemistry of soybeans, a leguminous plant that is very rich in protein. European industries were using natural soybean products as precursors for the manufacture of many drugs.

After receiving a doctorate degree in organic chemistry from the University of Vienna in 1931, Julian returned to Howard University and was promoted to full professor. After a disagreement with university officials in 1932, he left and went to DePauw University as a research fellow and an organic chemistry teacher. He continued researching synthesis methods of compounds from plants in collaboration with Josef Pikl, a colleague from the University of Vienna. He focused on the structure and synthesis of a substance isolated from the Calabar bean, *physostigmine*, a muscle relaxant used to treat glaucoma, an eye disease characterized by increased pressure of the fluid within the eye. By relaxing the muscles around the eye, excess fluid is able to drain away, relieving pressure on the optic nerve. Julian's goal was to create the substance physostigmine in the laboratory, which ultimately would be much cheaper than extracting the natural substance from plants. He had made progress in identifying the precursors that led to the formation of physostigmine when a renowned chemist, Sir Robert Robinson of Oxford University, announced results that differed from Julian's. This did not prevent Julian from confidently proceeding to publish his results in a 1934 issue of the *Journal of the American Chemical Society*, "Studies in the Indole Series. II. The Alkylation of 1-Methyl-3-Formyloxindole and a Synthesis of the Basic Ring Structure of Physostigmine." He included a statement concluding that Robinson was in error, arousing attention among his fellow chemists. In 1935, Julian successfully synthesized physostigmine, proving his method was correct and establishing a name for himself in the field of organic chemistry.

Soybean Chemist Extraordinaire

The year 1935 was also significant because Julian was appointed director of research of the Soya Products Division for the Glidden Company in Chicago. He had been denied a professorship at DePauw and became frustrated with the continued racial discrimination. He was the first African American in the United States to direct a major industrial laboratory. Later he also became the director of research for Glidden's Durkee Famous Foods Division and manager of the Fine Chemicals Division. In December of 1935, he married Anna Johnson, who held a Ph.D. in sociology. They had two children together, Percy Lavon, Jr., and Faith Roselle.

Glidden manufactured several products including paint. At Glidden, Julian extracted compounds from soybeans and developed new uses for soybean proteins. The company was interested in synthesizing substances that would act similarly to the protein casein, which is a protein found in milk and was also used in industrial processes such as waterproofing materials, making paints, and coating paper so ink would not be absorbed but still stick to the surface. Julian developed a method for extracting a protein from soybeans that was very similar to casein, greatly increasing Glidden's earnings. Another product that Julian developed from soy protein was Aero-Foam, a flame retardant used by the military to fight gasoline or oil fires, for which water is ineffective. The leftover soy meal was sold as feed for livestock and poultry. Julian's lab then developed food products including oils for making margarine, salad dressings, and soy lecithin (used as an emulsifier by the food industry). Soybean oil is *cholesterol*-free and low in saturated fats, making it a popular choice among health-conscious consumers. Tofu is a protein-rich food made from soybean curd and pressed into blocks; it is a primary source of protein in eastern Asia.

Steroidal Syntheses

Other major accomplishments from the Julian lab resulted from his research on *sterols*. Back at DePauw, while trying to isolate a companion alkaloid of physostigmine from the Calabar bean, Julian extracted the oil and washed it with acid. A few weeks later he noticed that crystals had formed in the oil. Analysis showed the crystals were hydrates of the sterol stigmasterol. Sterols are a type of chemical, mostly unsaturated alcohols like cholesterol, that are found in plant and animal tissues. The body uses sterols to build *steroid* hormones that play important roles in everything from the regulation of metabolic activity to sexual maturation and development. Sterols were needed by the pharmaceutical industry to act as a base from which steroid hormones could be synthesized. Sterols could be purified

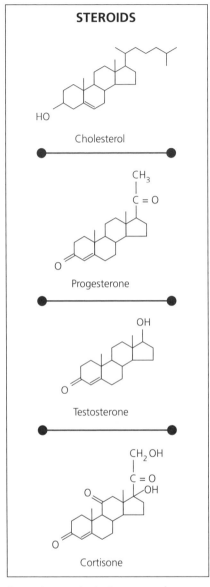

STEROIDS

Cholesterol

Progesterone

Testosterone

Cortisone

Progesterone, testosterone, and cortisone are all steroids derived from the four-ringed molecule cholesterol.

from the bile of slaughtered animals, but the contemporary methodology required thousands of animals to yield only enough of the substance to treat one patient for one year—and it was terribly expensive. Julian knew that it would be beneficial to be able to extract the sterols from soybean oil, but they were difficult to separate. He became preoccupied with other matters at Glidden.

One day in 1940, when Julian was notified that a tank of soybean oil had been contaminated with water and had formed a white mass, he remembered the valuable crystals that had formed in his Calabar bean oil. Investigation of the oily mass led to the development of a method for extracting the sterols from soybean oil by first converting it into a porous foam. He then figured out how to best synthesize the steroid hormones *progesterone* and *testosterone* from the sterols in the laboratory. Progesterone is a hormone produced in high levels during pregnancy to maintain the lining of the uterus, among other things. At the time, it was used to prevent miscarriages, and today it is used to treat reproductive system problems such as premenstrual symptoms and irregular menstruation and is a component of some birth control pills. Testosterone is produced by males and is necessary to stimulate sexual development, maintain fertility, and generate a normal sex drive. These hormones previously had been purified in tiny quantities from hundreds of pounds of testicles or ovaries or produced from cholesterol purified from the brains and spinal cords of cattle, so Julian's discovery was a tremendous advancement.

In 1948, researchers discovered that *cortisone* alleviated arthritis symptoms. Cortisone is another steroid hormone, structurally related to progesterone and testosterone. Produced by the adrenal cortex, the outer portion of the adrenal glands (the adrenal glands are located on top of the kidneys), cortisone regulates the levels of salt and sugar and helps the body respond appropriately to stressful situations. This hormone also reduces inflammation and thus is an effective treatment for rheumatoid arthritis, a painful condition resulting from inflammation of the lining of the joints. Unfortunately, it was very expensive to purify from bile acids, costing hundreds of dollars for a fraction of an ounce. Julian figured out how to obtain it synthetically at a fraction of the cost starting from pregnenolone, a substance that could be extracted from soybeans. From pregnenolone, he synthesized cortexolone (also known as Reichstein's Substance S), a molecule that differed from cortisone by a single missing oxygen atom. In 1952, the Upjohn Company determined that the missing oxygen could be added microbiologically, and the demand for supplies of pregnenolone and cortexolone rose sharply. Julian's synthesis of cortexolone benefited many patients suffering from a variety of maladies by making treatment widely available and affordable. Synthetic cortisone is also used in a variety of topical ointments used to treat itching caused by insect bites and poison ivy.

In 1950, Percy Julian was named Chicagoan of the Year, but he still fought discrimination. His house, in the white neighborhood of Oak Park, an all-white suburb of Chicago, was set on fire before he moved in. He had to threaten legal action in order to have his water turned on. After the family moved in, dynamite was thrown in his yard, landing below his children's bedroom window. In 1951, he was refused admittance into an exclusive Chicago club where a private

Chemical Messengers

Hormones are chemical messengers produced by organisms to relay signals between different structures of the organism. In animals, hormones coordinate growth, development, metabolism, and reproduction. Plants also produce hormones that regulate their growth. Animal hormones usually are secreted into the bloodstream and carried throughout the entire body, but the hormones only act on specific targets. For example, calcitonin is a hormone that regulates calcium levels in the blood. Though produced by the thyroid gland, it is secreted into the bloodstream and travels throughout the body until it finds and binds a specific receptor on a target cell. Calcitonin's targets are bone tissue, which responds by increasing calcium deposition; the intestines, which reduce their calcium uptake; and the kidneys, which reduce cal-

luncheon for recognized scientists and industrialists was being held. Yet Julian never backed down, and he became an outspoken defender of civil rights.

A Humane Scientist

In 1954, when another chemist discovered that Mexican yams were an even better source of sterols than soybeans, Julian established his own chemical company, Julian Laboratories, in Oak Park, with a factory and a farm in Mexico City, Mexico. Julian Laboratories specialized in manufacturing intermediates from wild Mexican yams for the industrial production of steroids. One of their major products was cortisone, but Julian also developed methods for producing other drugs and intermediate products from the yam. He sold the manufacturing plant in 1961 for $2.3 million to the American company Smith, Kline, and French (today GlaxoSmithKline) and cium reabsorption. As a result, the calcium level of the bloodstream is lowered.

Hormones generally are classified in two main categories: protein or steroid. Protein hormones are large molecules made of chains of amino acids. They bind to receptors on the outside of their target cells and effect an immediate response. Examples of protein hormones include insulin, which is involved in regulation of blood sugar levels, and growth hormone, which stimulates growth and metabolism. Steroid hormones are structurally similar and are all based on the four-ringed molecule cholesterol. Because they are much smaller than protein hormones and are not water-soluble, they can pass through cellular membranes to bind specific receptors located inside cells. This type of chemical messenger usually affects gene expression, and the response is slower and longer lasting than the action of protein hormones. Examples of steroid hormones include the female sex hormones estrogen and progesterone; the male sex hormone testosterone; glucocorticoids, which raise blood glucose levels; and mineralocorticoids, which regulate levels of sodium and potassium.

used the money to found two small companies, the Julian Research Institute and Julian Associates in Franklin Park, Illinois. He continued to direct the businesses until his death.

In 1974, Julian was diagnosed with liver cancer. Though his health weakened, he continued to consult for Smith, Kline, and French on the uses of organic compounds. Julian died at age 76, on April 19, 1975, in Waukegan, Illinois. At his funeral, Julian was described as a complete human whose life works involved healing the body and building societal bridges. In the year following his death, his wife made a donation to DePauw to establish the Julian Memorial Scholarship Fund and the Julian Memorial Chemistry Fund.

In 1947, the National Association for the Advancement of Colored People awarded Julian the Spingarn Medal for outstanding achievement by a black American in any honorable field of human endeavor. Julian also received 19 honorary doctorate degrees from universities including Northwestern, Michigan State, and Oberlin College. He was awarded the Distinguished Service Award from the Phi Beta Kappa Association for his work with cortexolone and synthetic cortisone. In 1968, he was awarded the American Institute of Chemists' Chemical Pioneer Award, which recognizes chemists who have made outstanding contributions that have had a major impact on advances in chemical science and industry. Julian belonged to several learned societies including the American Chemical Society and the American Association for the Advancement of Science, and just one year before his death, he was elected to the National Academy of Sciences. Several schools and academic buildings bear his name, and in 1990 he became one of the first African Americans to be elected to the National Inventors Hall of Fame. In 1994, the United States Postal Service sold stamps bearing his image.

In 1964, Professor Luke E. Steiner of Oberlin College celebrated Julian as "a man who illustrates the general usefulness of an educated mind." Indeed, despite racial barriers, Julian's brilliance and expertise raised him from the position of a student who was denied a teaching assistantship to become a professor, then a director of research for a major corporation, and eventually founder and president of his own companies. Though immensely successful, he was driven by the humane objective of making medical treatments available to all who needed them. Julian's research made an impact on the chemical industry by developing methods to cheaply synthesize substances used to treat debilitating conditions such as glaucoma and arthritis. Many benefited. His ingenuity also led to the discovery of many novel industrial uses of plant products, including new methods of food production and the manufacture of many chemical intermediates.

CHRONOLOGY

1899	Percy Julian is born in Montgomery, Alabama on April 11
1916	Graduates from the State Normal School at the top of his class
1920	Graduates as valedictorian and receives a bachelor's degree in chemistry from DePauw University in Greencastle, Indiana

1920–22	Teaches chemistry at Fisk University in Nashville, Tennessee
1923	Earns a master's degree in organic chemistry from Harvard University
1923–26	Continues studying biophysics and organic chemistry at Harvard University
1926–27	Teaches at West Virginia State College
1928	Becomes an associate professor and head of the chemistry department at Howard University in Washington, D.C.
1929	Receives a fellowship from the Rockefeller Foundation General Education Board and travels to Vienna to study alkaloid synthesis with Ernst Späth
1931	Receives a doctorate degree in organic chemistry from the University of Vienna and is promoted to full professor after returning to Howard University. He starts studying the structure and synthesis of physostigmine
1932	Resigns from Howard University and becomes a research fellow and organic chemistry teacher at DePauw University
1934	Presents research on the synthesis of physostigmine to the American Chemical Society
1935	Successfully synthesizes physostigmine
1936	Becomes the first African American to direct a major industrial laboratory when the Glidden Company in Chicago names him director of research for the Soya Products Division. Extracts vegetable protein from the soybean
1940	Develops procedure for extracting sterols from soybean oil, leading to the synthesis of progesterone and testosterone
1948	Synthesizes cortexolone, a precursor to cortisone
1954	Leaves Glidden and opens Julian Laboratories, Inc., in Chicago and the Laboratorios Julian de Mexico in Mexico City, Mexico
1961	Sells Chicago plant to Smith, Kline, and French (now GlaxoSmithKline) but remains president until 1964

1964	Founds the Julian Research Institute and Julian Associates, Inc., in Franklin Park, Illinois
1975	Dies from liver cancer on April 19, at age 76, in Waukegan, Illinois
1990	Is elected to the National Inventors Hall of Fame

FURTHER READING

Biographical Memoirs. National Academy of Sciences. Vol. 52. Washington, D.C.: National Academy of Sciences, 1980. Memoir of Julian's life and accomplishments written by a distinguished colleague.

Garraty, John A., and Mark C. Carnes, eds. *American National Biography*, Vol. 12. New York: Oxford University Press, 1999. Brief accounts of the lives and works of famous Americans in encyclopedia format.

Hayden, Robert C. *7 African American Scientists.* Frederick, Md.: Twenty First Century Books, 1992. Examines the lives and achievements of seven African Americans who have made significant contributions to various scientific fields. Appropriate for young adults.

Holmes, Frederic L., ed. *Dictionary of Scientific Biography.* Vol. 17, Supp. 2. New York: Scribner, 1990. Good source for facts concerning personal background and scientific accomplishments but assumes basic knowledge of science.

Jenkins, Edward S., ed. *American Black Scientists and Inventors.* Washington, D.C.: National Science Teachers Association, 1975. Describes the background, achievements, and personalities of 12 African-American scientists and inventors.

Krapp, Kristine M., ed. *Notable Black American Scientists.* Detroit, Mich.: Gale Research, 1999. Brief biographies of approximately 250 African Americans who have made contributions to the sciences.

"Percy Lavon Julian and Carl Djerassi." Chemical Heritage Foundation, 2000. Available online. URL: http://www.chem heritage.org/EducationalServices/chemach/ppb/ld.html. Accessed February 5, 2005. Part of the chemical achievers biographical profile series aimed at middle and high school students.

Smith, Jessie Carney, ed. *Black Heroes.* Detroit, Mich.: Visible Ink Press, 2001. Profiles 150 individuals who have significantly influenced African-American culture, not limited to scientists.

Linus Pauling

(1901–1994)

Linus Pauling won scientific acclaim for his eloquent description of the nature of chemical bonds. (© *The Nobel Foundation*)

Description of the Nature of the Chemical Bond

Modern scientists usually concentrate on a highly specialized topic for their doctoral dissertation research; unfortunately, breadth of knowledge sometimes is sacrificed to attain this focused expertise. One American scientist, Linus Pauling, embraced a wide range of interests, from mineralogy to quantum mechanics and immunology to evolution, but most of his research related to the structure of molecules. Pauling was the first to describe a molecular basis for a disease, sickle-cell anemia, and was a huge proponent of vitamin C for treating the common cold, but he was most famous for his work on chemical bonding. His descriptions of the forces responsible for holding atoms together to create molecules won him the Nobel Prize in chemistry in 1954. Pauling became a controversial figure when he actively campaigned against nuclear testing, and the U.S. government accused him of being a communist and refused him permission for international travel. The rest of the world viewed him differently, and he was awarded the Nobel Peace Prize for 1962, becoming the only person to win two unshared Nobel Prizes. Many consider Pauling to be the greatest chemist of the 20th century.

Boy Professor

Linus Carl Pauling was born on February 28, 1901, in Portland, Oregon. His father, Herman Henry William Pauling, was a pharmacist who died from a perforated ulcer when Linus was only nine, leaving his mother, Lucy Isabelle ("Belle") Darling Pauling, to raise him and his two younger sisters. Linus was a voracious reader from an early age, and by the time his father passed away he had already read Charles Darwin's *On the Origin of Species* and the Bible. As a young adult, he collected insects and minerals and explored the wonders of chemistry with a childhood friend, performing simple experiments, setting off stink bombs, and making explosions. Linus entered Oregon Agricultural College (OAC, now Oregon State University) in Corvallis without having obtained a high school diploma because he lacked the required history courses. He studied chemical engineering and though he worked during the summers testing the composition of asphalt used to pave highways, financial difficulties forced him into the decision to leave school after only two years.

After hearing of Pauling's situation, the OAC faculty hired the 19-year-old as an instructor of quantitative analysis, a course he had just completed the year before. His pupils found his lectures entertaining and informative, and students vied to get into the classes taught by the "Boy Professor." The following year Pauling resumed his studies, graduating with a bachelor of science degree in chemical engineering in 1922. During college, independent reading of current chemistry journals brought to Pauling's attention the ideas put forth by chemists Gilbert Newton Lewis and Irving Langmuir on the forces that held molecules together. Lewis and Langmuir proposed that elements were held together by the natural tendency of atoms to attain a stable structure with eight electrons in their outermost, or valence, shell. For example, if an atom had only seven electrons in its valence shell, it tended to share an electron pair with an atom that had only one, forming a covalent bond and providing each atom with a complete octet.

Wanting to learn more about chemical bonding, Pauling proceeded to the California Institute of Technology (Caltech) where he began studies toward a doctorate in physical chemistry. The offer of a generous stipend and the recent hiring of internationally known Arthur Amos Noyes, who was in the process of transforming the chemistry department into a renowned research center, attracted Pauling to Caltech. His dissertation research under Roscoe Dickinson involved the use of X-ray diffraction to study the structures of inorganic crystals. Dickinson had earned his Ph.D. only two years before and, as the resident expert in *X-ray crystallography*, was qualified to teach Pauling the new and complicated technique. Pauling measured bond angles and distances in crystals of the mineral molybdenite, solving its structure for his thesis. He exhibited a natural ability to combine experimental and theoretical chemistry, and he intuitively recognized the relationship between the structure of molecules and their chemical behavior. By the time he earned his Ph.D. in chemistry in 1925, with minors in mathematics and physics, he had published 12 scientific papers on inorganic crystal structure. During graduate school he married Ava Helen Miller, one of his former students, to whom he remained married for almost 60 years and with whom he had four children.

After obtaining his doctorate, a Guggenheim Fellowship took Pauling to the Institute of Theoretical Physics in Munich, Germany, where he mastered quantum mechanics, the burgeoning field of physics that attempted to explain the structure and behavior of matter at the subatomic level. Pauling met many influential physicists while in Europe, including Arnold Sommerfield, who directed the institute, Erwin Schrödinger, Max Born, Werner Heisenberg, J. Robert Oppenheimer, and Niels Bohr. Pauling established a name for himself by publishing an article describing atomic properties using wave mechanics in the prestigious journal *Proceedings of the Royal Society of London* in 1927. While writing the article, "The Theoretical Prediction of the Physical Properties of Many-Electron Atoms and Ions: Mole Refraction, Diamagnetic Susceptibility and Extension in Space," Pauling realized that quantum mechanics may reveal the answers to many questions regarding atomic behavior. He also recognized the significance of the work done by two German physicists working with Schrödinger, Walter Heitler and Fritz London, who used wave mechanics to model chemical bonding. They demonstrated that as atoms approached one another, their electrons became attracted to each other's positively charged nucleus and rapidly jumped back and forth. At the same time, the positively charged nuclei repelled one another, resulting in a defined bond length between the two atoms.

Pauling's Rules and Chemical Bonding Theory

Upon returning to Caltech, the 26-year-old rising star became an assistant professor of theoretical chemistry and applied his newly adopted manner of looking at matter and energy to chemistry. He was promoted to associate professor in less than two years. Pauling quickly established himself as an expert in structural chemistry and made several early achievements at Pasadena, publishing almost 50 papers on X-ray crystallography and quantum chemistry during his first five years on the faculty. Using both quantum mechanics and experimental data from inorganic crystals, he proposed that one could approximate the distances between atoms by simply adding the radii of the participating *cations* and *anions*. The values for ionic radii that he determined are still commonly used today, as are his values for covalent and van der Waals radii. He outlined a set of guidelines concerning the stability of crystal structures, making it easier for chemists to test the correctness of possible structures for complex ionic or covalent crystals. The rules described in "The

Principles Determining the Structure of Complex Ionic Crystals," published in the *Journal of the American Chemical Society* in 1929, became known as "Pauling's rules" and further substantiated his international reputation.

As his interest increased in how atoms combined to form molecules, Pauling used quantum mechanics to explore exhaustively the formation and characteristics of chemical bonds. In 1931, he published his first paper of a series titled "The Nature of the Chemical Bond" that led to his 1939 publication of a book by a similar name, *The Nature of the Chemical Bond and the Structure of Molecules and Crystals: An Introduction to Modern Structural Chemistry.* This work applied quantum mechanics to concepts including *hybridization, resonance,* and *electronegativity* and became one of the most influential texts in scientific history. In recognition of his brilliant accomplishments, Caltech promoted Pauling to full professor in 1931, and the American Chemical Society named him the best young chemist in the nation by awarding him their Langmuir Prize. In 1933, he became the youngest person to be elected to the National Academy of Sciences.

The valence bond (VB) theory and the molecular *orbital* (MO) theory were attempts to explain the sharing of electrons among atoms in a molecule. The VB approach considers individual atoms with their own electron orbitals coming together to form covalent bonds, whereas the MO approach collectively considers all of the atomic nuclei comprising the molecule encircled by sets of molecular orbitals. Pauling seemed to favor the VB approach, but it could not explain the quadrivalency of the atom carbon, its ability to provide four equal-energy orbitals to form four equivalent bonds with other atoms. To remedy this, he developed the concept of hybridization, the combination of the outer, or valence, orbitals of an atom to form hybrid orbitals. Mixing the orbitals changes their spatial arrangements and energies. He gave molecules three dimensions and imagined that atoms could change their shapes to form stronger bonds, a notion that was difficult for some chemists to accept.

Pauling used the idea of resonance to explain the stability of chemical bonds, in particular the carbon-carbon bonds of aromatic molecules such as benzene (C_6H_6). In 1857, the German organic

Hybridization in the Special Case of Carbon

To better understand the concept of hybridization, consider the atom carbon, atomic number 6. Two electrons occupy the lowest energy level consisting of one s orbital. The four remaining valence electrons occupy the next energy level, consisting of one s orbital and three p orbitals. If each of the four valence electrons

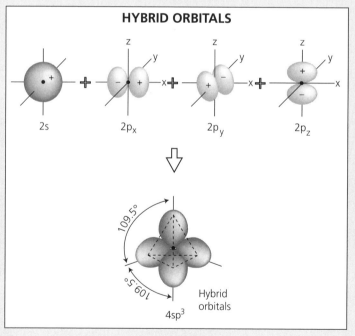

HYBRID ORBITALS

Hybrid orbitals

$4sp^3$

One $2s$ and three $2p$ orbitals combine to form four sp^3 hybrid orbitals, allowing carbon to participate in four equivalent bonds with other atoms. The labels $2s$ and $2p$ indicate the energy levels and subshells of the participating electrons. The subscripts x, y, and z refer to the probable locations of the electrons within the p subshell.

occupied a different orbital in the second energy level, the bond energies and lengths would not be equivalent. Combining the one low-energy s orbital with the three slightly higher-energy p orbitals gives four equivalent sp^3 orbitals with a weighted average energy. The number of hybrid orbitals must equal the number of combined original orbitals.

When one carbon atom binds with four hydrogen atoms, methane (CH_4) is formed. Hybridization explains why all the carbon *hydrogen bond* lengths, strengths, and angles are equal, forming a perfect tetrahedron.

chemist Friedrich Kekulé proposed that carbon was tetravalent and described the structure of benzene as a ring with alternating single and double bonds that rapidly interconverted. This can be depicted as a hexagon with alternating single and double bonds, followed by a double-sided arrow and another hexagon with single bonds replacing the first structure's double bonds and vice versa. Pauling used quantum mechanics to show that benzene was really an intermediate structure like a hybrid orbital. The resonant forms do not rapidly alternate in a dynamic equilibrium, but the true structure lies somewhere in between the two, making the distribution of electrons difficult to depict.

A third concept that Pauling explored in *The Nature of the Chemical Bond* was electronegativity, defined as the power of an atom within a molecule to attract electrons to itself. (*Electron affinity* is the power of a free atom to draw electrons to itself.) He used this concept to estimate bond energies and to estimate *dipole moments* in polar covalent bonds of molecules in which one atom is slightly more positive than the other. Dipole moments are apparent in certain molecular geometric arrangements. Electronegativities may also be used to predict the character of chemical bonds. Ionic bonds result when electrons are donated by one atom and accepted by another, whereas covalent bonds form when two atoms each

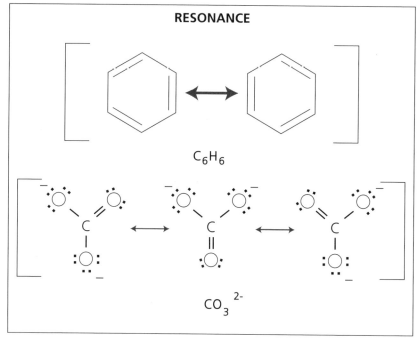

In some ions or molecules the valence electrons are delocalized, spread over more than two atoms, and the electronic structure must be represented as a resonance hybrid of the contributing structures.

donate an electron to a shared pair. Most bonds are intermediate between the two extremes of ionic and covalent. The greater the difference in electronegativities of two elements, the more likely their atoms will form a characteristically ionic compound; the lower the difference in electronegativities, the more likely the compound will be covalent.

The Structure and Function of Biological Molecules

About 1934, Pauling's interests shifted toward proteins, biomolecules consisting of long chains of 20 different amino acids. Proteins are the major structural building blocks of cells, and they perform most of the cellular work as enzymes that catalyze, or speed up, the rate of biological reactions. The first protein Pauling studied was hemoglobin, an iron-containing protein that carries oxygen (O_2) inside red blood cells by circulation. He determined that the oxygen molecule formed a covalent bond with the iron atom of hemoglobin using principles of magnetic susceptibility, a measurement of how easily sediments are magnetized when subjected to a magnetic field based on the iron content.

Pauling was the first to recognize and emphasize the structural, and therefore functional, significance of hydrogen bonding in proteins and other biomolecules. Hydrogen bonds are weak chemical attractions between a partially positive hydrogen atom and a partially negative atom of another molecule or a different portion of the same molecule. While the strength of an individual hydrogen bond is approximately one-twentieth of a covalent bond, the collective action of numerous hydrogen bonds holds together tightly two molecules or different portions of the same molecule. After amino acids are joined together to create a long polypeptide chain during protein synthesis, the chain folds back on itself and sometimes combines with other polypeptides to form a unique conformation called the native form. Subjecting proteins to heat or acid causes them to denature, or unfold. If the treatment is mild, the unfolding may be reversible; if the conditions are harsh, the protein may be irreversibly damaged and will no longer function. Pauling examined this process and concluded, in 1936, that mild denaturation and then renaturation involved the breaking and reformation of hydrogen bonds, whereas irreversible denaturation was associated with the breakage of covalent linkages that resulted in inactive proteins.

Pauling also studied *antibodies*, proteins synthesized by the immune system that recognize *antigens*, usually other proteins. Antibodies are highly specific, meaning they only recognize one certain antigen and no others, a characteristic that intrigued Pauling. He formulated a theory based on complementarity, stating that the atoms of the antigen attracted complementary parts of the antibody, an idea that holds true today. He also incorrectly assumed that all antibodies were made of the polypeptide chains with the same sequence but folded differently to conform to their specific antigens.

In 1937, Caltech named Pauling the chair of the division of chemistry and chemical engineering, and the department enjoyed a renowned international reputation and a magnificent new bioorganic chemistry building outfitted with modern equipment. Pauling worked 12-hour days, seven days a week, and he loved his work. In 1941, his doctor diagnosed him with Bright's disease, an ailment that prevents the kidneys from filtering the blood properly. He restored his health over several months by grossly modifying his diet—severely restricting his salt and protein intake and relying on vitamin and mineral supplements. Pearl Harbor was attacked in December, and Pauling's research for the next few years centered on war work, for which he received, in 1948, the Presidential Medal for Merit, the highest civilian honor in the United States. After the war and with the support of his wife, Pauling added his voice to the moral debate over the atomic bomb and to the campaign to place control of nuclear weaponry in civilian hands. His outspokenness and firm stance caused him problems later.

Protein Conformations

In 1947, Pauling temporarily moved his family to England, where he served as the Eastman Visiting Professor at Oxford. That same year he published an enormously successful college textbook, *General Chemistry*. Before returning home, while recovering from one of many serious colds he would suffer in the following decades, he started thinking about the structure of alpha-keratin, a protein found in hair and horny tissues.

Pauling had spent time on this protein a decade earlier, but new developments in the field convinced him he might make better progress solving the structure this time around. Believing the structure was helical, he used paper models to construct the polypeptide chain and rotated all the single bonds, except the rigid peptide bond, in a stepwise manner until he achieved a helical structure that agreed with the angles and interatomic distances calculated from X-ray crystallography performed by Robert B. Corey (also from Caltech) and colleagues. Referred to as an *alpha-helix*, this twisted arrangement involved hydrogen bonding between the –NH group of one amino acid and the carbonyl oxygen of another positioned four amino acids farther down the chain, with the carbonyl groups running parallel to the axis of the helix. He published a series of

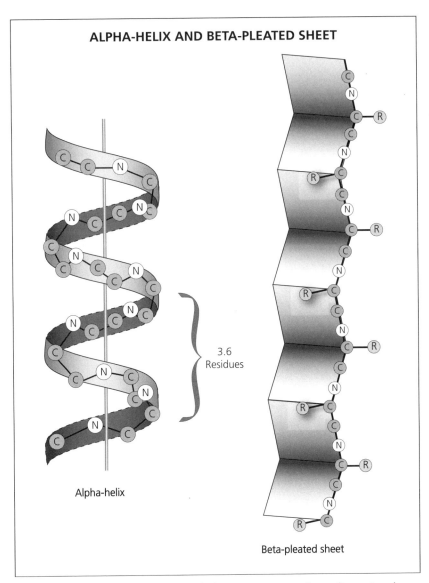

ALPHA-HELIX AND BETA-PLEATED SHEET

3.6
Residues

Alpha-helix

Beta-pleated sheet

The alpha-helix and the beta-pleated sheet are common three-dimensional conformations of polypeptide chains stabilized by hydrogen bonding.

papers during the period 1950–51 describing this motif and others; a remarkable seven papers appeared in the same May 1951 issue of *Proceedings of the National Academy of Sciences.* Another structure he described that has withstood the test of time was the *beta-pleated sheet*, consisting of pairs of polypeptide chains lying side by side and stabilized by hydrogen bonds between the carbonyl oxygen on one chain and the –NH group on the other chain. Chains that run in the same direction are called parallel, and chains that run in the reverse direction are called antiparallel. Since Pauling's discovery, biochemists have identified these motifs in thousands of proteins.

Though Pauling was a gifted chemist, he was not right about everything. One pride-damaging blunder was his proposal for the structure of DNA that consisted of a triple helix and protonated phosphate groups. James Watson, a codiscoverer of the correct double helical model, claimed that Pauling's obvious mistake was crucial in stimulating him to solve the structure within a matter of weeks. Pauling's error, however, did not take away from what he had already accomplished. In 1954, Pauling received the Nobel Prize in chemistry for his research into the nature of the chemical bond and its application to the elucidation of the structure of complex substances. He was pleased to be recognized for such a broadly described accomplishment that seemed to encompass everything he had done during his career.

A Molecular Disease

Sickle-cell anemia is a hereditary disease in which the normally flat, disc-shaped red blood cells adopt a deformed, sickled configuration, causing them to become wedged in tiny vessels, blocking the flow of blood. The crescent-shaped blood cells also have a shorter lifespan, thus less oxygen is delivered to the tissues of afflicted individuals, causing a variety of symptoms including fatigue, pain, an increased risk for infections, and even death. Pauling thought that the disease might be caused by an altered sequence of amino acids in the protein hemoglobin affecting the protein's structure and, consequently, the structure of the red blood cells. *Electrophoresis* is a technique in which substances placed in a semisolid matrix are subjected to an electric current, resulting in separation based on differences in their electrical charge. In 1949, Pauling used electrophoresis to demonstrate that normal and abnormal hemoglobin traveled at different rates in an electric field, suggesting a difference in the protein molecules. This was the first description of a disease caused by a change

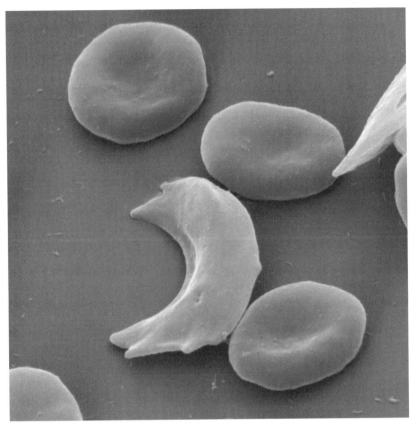

Characterized by distorted, sickle-shaped blood cells, sickle-cell anemia results from the mutation of a single amino acid in the hemoglobin protein. *(Eye of Science/Photo Researchers, Inc.)*

in protein structure. His astounding finding earned him honorary degrees from Cambridge, Oxford, and London Universities, nomination for the presidency of the National Academy of Sciences, and the presidency of the American Chemical Society. In 1956, Vernon Ingram and J. A. Hunt, working at the Medical Research Council Unit at the Cavendish Laboratory at the University of Cambridge, sequenced hemoglobin and found that the abnormal hemoglobin molecule had the amino acid valine instead of glutamic acid; a change in one single amino acid caused the disease.

The determination that sickle-cell anemia was a molecular disease led Pauling to propose, with Emile Zuckerkandl in 1962, the concept of a *molecular clock*. Sequencing of proteins had become commonplace, and they observed a correlation between the number of amino acid residues altered in the same protein of two different species and the evolutionary distance between them. For example, horses and humans diverged long before gorillas and humans. Horse and human hemoglobin chains that were 150 amino acids long differed by 18 residues, whereas gorilla and human chains differed by only two amino acids. Pauling suggested that the rate of change of a protein was constant over time and that protein sequencing data could be used to estimate when two species diverged. Modern evolutionary biologists compare nucleic acid sequence information to accomplish the same goal.

Antibomb Activism

Since World War II, Pauling had used his scientific status to oppose the testing and use of nuclear weapons. He felt his unusual perspective as a scientist on the effects of radioactive fallout obliged him to make a strong and public stance, which drew attention from the U.S. government. He joined organizations such as the Emergency Committee of Atomic Scientists and circulated petitions protesting the development of nuclear weapons. In a national atmosphere where people believed in a huge communist conspiracy against which nuclear weapons were the only defense, those who protested their use were considered communists themselves or traitors. The United States denied Pauling's application for a passport to lecture at a Royal Society meeting in 1952, an action that the outraged scientific world viewed as an insult. Other requests also were denied, and colleagues and friends began to withdraw from him.

By the time Pauling's Nobel Prize was announced in November of 1954, the United States had wedged itself into the embarrassing position of reluctantly having to allow Pauling, who was appreciated everywhere but his home country, the permission to travel to Sweden to accept the award or risk an international uproar. Pauling was instrumental in collecting thousands of signatures on a petition to end nuclear bomb testing presented to the secretary general of the United Nations in 1958. He also published the antibomb book

No More War! that year and resigned his position as chair of the chemistry division under pressure from Caltech's president. The Soviet Union, United Kingdom, and the United States did halt testing temporarily, and eventually the U.S. public started hearing Pauling's message about the dangers of nuclear weapons. For his efforts to end nuclear testing and for peace, the Nobel Committee awarded Pauling the Nobel Peace Prize for 1962.

Belief in a Miracle Vitamin

The focus of Pauling's research shifted away from traditional chemistry toward the molecular basis of mental diseases, making his colleagues unhappy. Some expressed concern that his attention to antiwar activism and the dangers of radioactive fallout left him out of touch with chemistry. Feeling misunderstood and unsupported, Pauling left Caltech after four decades and went to work at the Center for the Study of Democratic Institutions, a liberal think tank in Santa Barbara, California. In 1967, he became a research professor of chemistry at the University of California at San Diego, and then two years later he moved to Stanford University, from which he retired as a professor emeritus of chemistry in 1974. The lack of a stable work location interfered with his ability to do research.

Colds had always troubled Pauling, and in 1966 he had begun consuming three grams of vitamin C, also called *ascorbic acid*, each day. To put this in perspective, consider the recommended daily allowance is currently 60 milligrams, 50 times less than he was taking. He claimed to have felt healthier and that his colds were less frequent and less severe. To the dismay of the medical establishment, he started publicly preaching the benefits of taking mega doses of vitamin C. In 1970, he published *Vitamin C and the Common Cold*, a book that emphasized studies that showed a positive benefit from taking large amounts of vitamin C and refuted opposing studies. The book became a best seller, and consumers began purchasing large quantities of vitamin C to prevent and treat the common cold.

Pauling began collaborating with Scottish physician Ewan Cameron, who believed vitamin C was beneficial to cancer patients. They published a paper in the *Proceedings of the National Academy of*

Sciences in 1976 titled "Supplemental Ascorbate in the Supportive Treatment: Prolongation of Survival Times in Terminal Human Cancer," and a book in 1979 titled *Cancer and Vitamin C.* Again, the public embraced their claims, but the medical establishment was not pleased. The National Institutes of Health has conceded that a few studies suggest that taking vitamin C might prevent the onset or duration of a cold, but the majority of research shows no effect. No scientific studies have verified a beneficial effect of vitamin C on cancer.

In 1973, with the help of Arthur B. Robinson, Pauling established the Linus Pauling Institute of Science and Medicine in Palo Alto, California. In 1996, the institute moved to Oregon State University, where research currently focuses on heart disease, cancer, aging, and neurodegenerative diseases.

The death in 1981 of his wife of almost 60 years from stomach cancer devastated Pauling. He published another popular health book titled *How to Live Longer and Feel Better* (1986). He was diagnosed with prostate cancer in 1991. Though he lived for three more years taking massive amounts of vitamin C, he died on August 19, 1994, at his ranch in Big Sur, California.

Linus Pauling was a passionate, charming, conceited, and brilliant Renaissance man with an interest in and comprehension of numerous subjects. A master of chemistry, he had an extraordinary ability for building molecular models within his own head, as if he could see the actual atoms interacting with one another. To make it easier for the rest of the world to understand what came to him naturally, he condensed his expansive knowledge into a few simple rules to explain chemical bonding and predict molecular structures. Pauling's numerous and substantial contributions to the field of chemistry include his explanation of chemical bonding in terms of hybridization, character, and resonance, his elucidation of the architecture of proteins and other molecular structures, and his description of sickle-cell anemia as the first identified molecular disease. He also is credited with the foundation of molecular biology, molecular medicine, and even molecular evolution. While he was able to flawlessly merge physics and biology with chemistry and was an expert at combining theoretical and experimental data,

Pauling divulged that he was more pleased with his Nobel Peace Prize than his scientific discoveries. Learners in every field can benefit from the inspirational advice he gave to a group of students at the 1954 Nobel award ceremony in Stockholm, words he obviously took to heart himself:

> "When an old and distinguished person speaks to you, listen to him carefully and with respect—*but do not believe him. Never put your trust in anything but your own intellect.* Your elder, no matter whether he has gray hair or has lost his hair, no matter whether he is a Nobel Laureate, *may be wrong.* The world progresses, year by year, century by century, as the members of younger generations find out what was wrong among the things that their elders said. So you must always be skeptical—*always think for yourself.*"

CHRONOLOGY

1901	Linus Pauling is born on February 28 in Portland, Oregon
1917	Enters the chemical engineering program at Oregon Agricultural College (OAC)
1919–20	Teaches quantitative analysis at OAC
1922	Receives a bachelor's degree in chemical engineering from Oregon Agricultural College (OAC)
1925	Receives a doctorate degree in chemistry from the California Institute of Technology (Caltech)
1926–27	Studies quantum physics in Europe as a Guggenheim fellow
1927	Becomes assistant professor of theoretical chemistry at Caltech
1929	Becomes associate professor at Caltech and publishes a set of guidelines for determining the structures of complex crystals that become known as Pauling's Rules
1930–35	Works on explaining the nature of the chemical bond in terms of quantum mechanics

contains an understandable description of the technical information related to Pauling's work.

Nobelprize.org. "The Nobel Prize in Chemistry 1964." Available online. URL: http://nobelprize.org/chemistry/laureates/1954. Last modified June 16, 2000. Includes links to his biography, Nobel lecture, and other resources.

Olson, Richard, ed. *Biographical Encyclopedia of Scientists.* Vol. 4. New York: Marshall Cavendish, 1998. Clear, concise summary of major events in scientists' lives at an accessible level.

Dorothy Crowfoot Hodgkin

(1910–1994)

Dorothy Hodgkin was a pioneering X-ray crystallographer who continuously pushed the limits of the technique to decipher the three-dimensional structures of several biologically important molecules. (© *The Nobel Foundation*)

X-Ray Analysis of Biologically Important Molecules

The world would reach a technological standstill if scientists did not push to expand the capabilities of their methodology. A researcher must take risks to make groundbreaking advances; unfortunately, wasted time combined with possible failure and ridicule deters many from trying. Expert knowledge and years of experience can provide the courage and confidence necessary to assume a risky undertaking. Dorothy Hodgkin was a bold chemist interested in the structural analysis of biomolecules that others thought were too difficult to decipher. Understanding that structure determines function, Hodgkin helped establish a new approach to studying biomolecules while solving the molecular structures of cholesterol, penicillin, vitamin B_{12}, and insulin. Spanning seven decades, her pioneering research influenced the field of X-ray crystallography as well as chemistry and biochemistry.

A Sketchy but Worldly Education

Dorothy Mary Crowfoot was born in Cairo, Egypt, on May 12, 1910. At the time, her father, John Winter Crowfoot, worked as an administrator for the Egyptian Education Service, and in 1916, he became assistant director of education in the Sudan. Her mother, Grace Mary Hood Crowfoot, though never formally educated beyond finishing school, was an amateur botanist and became an expert in early weaving techniques and ancient textiles. Dorothy's family traveled a lot until World War I broke out, when Dorothy and two of her three younger sisters settled in Worthing, England, where a nanny and their paternal grandmother cared for them until Dorothy was eight. After having seen her parents only once during the preceding four years, the family settled close to relatives in the village of Geldeston, near Beccles, in northeastern Suffolk.

Dorothy had her first taste of chemistry when she was 10 years old and attended a local Parents National Educational Union class. Her chemistry booklet included experiments on growing copper sulfate and alum crystals that she found so captivating, she repeated them at home in a makeshift attic laboratory. Crystals are solids composed of atoms that are arranged in a regular, repeating pattern. At the Sir John Leman School in Beccles, which she attended from 1921 to 1928, Dorothy and a friend convinced the teachers to let them take the chemistry class, though it was supposed to be offered only to boys. Ironically, the teacher was female! Dorothy performed well enough to choose chemistry as her major in college. During this time, she also volunteered for various peace campaigns and began her lifelong association with the Labour Party, a democratic socialist party in Great Britain.

Dorothy took six months off from school during the period 1922–23 to visit her parents in the Sudan, where she visited the Wellcome Laboratory in Khartoum, met the director, the soil chemist A. F. Joseph, and learned to pan for gold. While practicing this new technique in her parents' backyard, she discovered shiny black chunks of a mineral that she analyzed and identified as ilmenite, iron titanium oxide. Her enthusiasm impressed Joseph, who gave her a professional kit for surveying and identifying minerals.

Upon graduation, Dorothy learned that she needed to learn Latin in addition to more mathematics and science if she wanted to study chemistry and crystallography in college. Extensive tutoring helped her prepare for the Oxford University entrance examination, which she passed. She then traveled to Jerusalem, where her father had become director of the British School of Archeology, and assisted her parents in excavating Byzantine churches by recording the patterns of the mosaic floors. She enjoyed the work and considered majoring in archaeology instead of chemistry.

Fascination with Crystals

At Somerville College for women at Oxford University, Dorothy developed a close relationship with Margery Fry, the principal of Somerville, and became fascinated by the relatively new field of X-ray crystallography. This technique is used by chemists to gain information about the atomic structure of molecules. Because atoms are much smaller than the wavelengths of visible light, they cannot diffract the light rays or be seen even with microscopes. The wavelengths of X-rays are much smaller and thus can be used to "see" atoms and molecules. The substance to be X-rayed must first be crystallized, a procedure in which the molecules become highly ordered, with regular spacing occurring between atoms in the arranged molecules. When bombarded with X-rays, the crystallized molecules diffract, or bend, the waves, which pass through the created spaces as through a grating, forming a unique pattern of blurry circles on photographic film. Examination and interpretation of

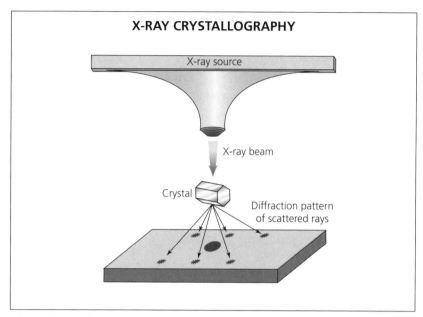

When a beam of X-rays is passed through a crystal, some waves are scattered in various directions, creating a pattern unique to the arrangements of atoms in the crystal.

the resulting patterns of spots requires a good understanding of chemistry, mathematics, and physics. Dorothy first learned about crystallography as a teenager, when her mother gave her two books based on William H. Bragg's Royal Institution Christmas Lectures for children, *Concerning the Nature of Things* (1925) and *Old Trades and New Knowledge* (1926). Bragg won the Nobel Prize in physics in 1915, which he shared with his son, William Lawrence Bragg, for their services in the analysis of crystal structure by means of X-rays. For her fourth-year research project, Dorothy synthesized and crystallized thallium dialkyl halides, then used X-ray diffraction to analyze the structures.

After Crowfoot graduated from Somerville College in 1932, her friend Joseph helped her obtain a position in the laboratory of John Desmond Bernal at Cambridge University, where she began graduate studies in X-ray crystallography. Bernal, a pioneer in the use of X-ray crystallography for the study of biological molecules, had been researching metals, but he started studying sterols around the time Crowfoot entered his laboratory. Scientists from all over the world sent Bernal crystals for analysis, and as his assistant Crowfoot had plenty of material on which she practiced her new skills. Though her Ph.D. thesis topic was the crystallographic investigation of steroid crystals, she also studied minerals, metals, other organic and inorganic molecules, proteins, and viruses. Between 1933 and 1936, Bernal listed her as coauthor on 12 scientific papers.

In 1934, Crowfoot saw a specialist about tenderness and inflammation in the joints of her hands. The doctor diagnosed her with rheumatoid arthritis, a painful condition caused by the body's attack on its own tissues that worsened throughout her life and ultimately deformed and crippled her. The depressing news of her disease only brought her down temporarily; when she returned to the lab that afternoon, she found that Bernal had successfully photographed a protein crystal of *pepsin*. He had figured out the trick was to keep the crystal wet and became the first to obtain a good X-ray photograph of a protein. Crowfoot soon immersed herself in

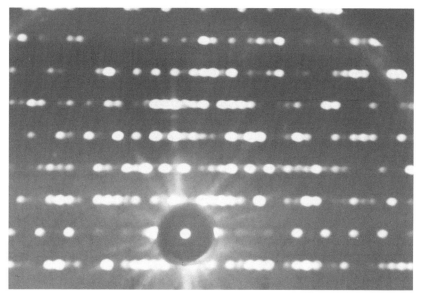

The white spots in this X-ray diffraction image reveal a unique pattern formed when X-rays pass through a protein crystal. The circular space and spot (lower center) is the pattern's center. *(Alfred Pasieka/Science Photo Library/Photo Researchers, Inc.)*

deciphering the photographs of pepsin, a digestive enzyme that hydrolyzes peptide bonds between amino acids of proteins in the stomach. According to the memoir written by Guy Dodson in the *Biographical Memoirs of Fellows of the Royal Society of London*, this was "the beginning of protein crystallography, and it was one of the most important scientific episodes in Dorothy's life."

Though she received financial assistance from her aunt and through a research grant from Cambridge, money was tight, so in 1933, Crowfoot accepted a research fellowship, to be held for one year at Cambridge and the second at Oxford. She reluctantly returned to Somerville College in 1934, not wanting to leave the intellectually stimulating environment of the lab at Cambridge, but she had to consider her future, and this position at Oxford could lead to a permanent job. She continued her doctoral studies on sterols and earned her Ph.D. in 1937. She remained at Oxford for the duration of her career.

In December of 1937, she married Thomas Hodgkin, a researcher and African political historian who was Fry's cousin. Like Bernal, Hodgkin was a member of the Communist Party. During the early years of their marriage, he organized adult education classes, and then later he became the director of the Institute of African Studies at the University of Ghana. During the years 1938–46, the Hodgkins had three children together, all of whom grew up to become respected professionals in their own fields. During her third pregnancy, Dorothy Hodgkin became the first woman at Oxford to receive paid maternity leave. She was a devoted, loving, patient mother who never complained about the demands of having children in a two-career family and worked hard to come home before dinnertime each night. She exhibited the same likable qualities to her colleagues and to the young scientists she mentored.

Primitive Lab, Superior Results

At Oxford, Hodgkin continued the research she began in Bernal's lab on sterols, a group of mostly unsaturated alcohols, including cholesterol, found in plant and animal tissues. The laboratory facilities available for her use at Oxford were much more primitive than those at Cambridge. In order to study a crystal with her polarizing microscope, she had to climb a rickety ladder to a gallery located just under the only window in her basement lab that allowed sufficient light for viewing. Though space and equipment were limited and hardly adequate, she obtained a series of grants and other financial support from the Rockefeller and Nuffield Foundations, and she did not let the pitiable working conditions affect the quality of her work.

Though Hodgkin studied over 100 steroids, she focused on cholesterol, a greasy molecule that acts as a precursor for the synthesis of many steroid hormones and is a component of animal cell membranes. The chemistry of cholesterol was understood, and the basic sterol formula was worked out, but no one knew how the atoms of carbon, hydrogen, and oxygen were arranged in three dimensions to form the functional molecule, and most thought it was too complicated for X-ray analysis. Liking a challenge, she deciphered the molecular structure of cholesteryl iodide and published it in the *Proceedings of the Royal Society* in 1945 as "The Crystal Structure of Cholesteryl Iodide." Cholesterol was the most complex organic structure solved to date and the first three-dimensional study of a biochemically important molecule.

The Structure of Penicillin

During World War II, Bernal started performing war research and donated his crystallographic equipment to Hodgkin. As the molecules she studied became increasingly complex, so did the mathematical calculations required to solve crystal structures. She gained access to an early type of computer, a Hollerith punch-card machine, to assist her with calculations. Hodgkin's graduate student, Barbara Rogers Low, wrote the first three-dimensional computer program and punched data into cards that then were inserted into the computer.

Hodgkin had switched her research focus to penicillin, a newly discovered, highly effective antibiotic made by the mold *Penicillium notatum*. She believed that learning its structure would

PENICILLIN

Beta-lactam ring

Hodgkin directly demonstrated that penicillin contained a beta-lactam ring.

help pharmaceutical companies to make the drug, which was in short supply. Different forms of the molecule crystallized in different ways, complicating its analysis. In 1945, after analyzing hundreds of spots on X-ray diffraction photographs, Hodgkin announced the arrangement of penicillin's atoms. Her research proved that penicillin contained a unique structure called a beta-lactam ring that was joined to a five-sided thiazolidine ring, an unusual attachment.

In 1946, Hodgkin helped form the International Union of Crystallography (IUCr) to encourage and facilitate the exchange of scientific information among all countries, including communist countries. The following year, Britain's foremost scientific organization, the Royal Society of London, elected her the third woman fellow. Oxford made her a university lecturer and demonstrator and increased her salary in 1946 but did not promote her to a university reader, a position similar to a full professor in the United States, until 1956 or provide her with a modern chemical crystallography laboratory until a few years later.

Too Complex for Chemical Analysis

The size of Hodgkin's research group grew with her fame, but she always tried to limit the number of workers to 10 to keep it manageable. After her discovery of the structure of penicillin, the drug company Glaxo sought her help in solving the structure of vitamin B_{12}, which had been discovered in 1926 but not isolated and purified until 1948. Vitamin B_{12} was necessary for the body to

synthesize red blood cells, and without adequate quantities people died from pernicious anemia. Pharmaceutical companies
wanted to manufacture the vitamin but needed to know its structure, which was too complex for chemical analysis and the standard methods of degradation and synthesis. When Glaxo brought
Hodgkin some crystals of vitamin B_{12} in 1948, she knew it would
require more than the four years it took to solve the structure of

The molecules Hodgkin chose for study became increasingly complex, as shown
by this depiction of vitamin B_{12}. "R" represents an additional nucleotide that is
present in the coenzyme.

penicillin, as it was much larger. The fact that no one had ever solved a structure so complicated did not deter her from consenting to the challenge. She was anxious to demonstrate the power of X-ray analysis.

Her initial studies suggested its structure was similar to porphyrin, a flat ring made of four smaller rings called pyrroles, found in hemoglobin. Others who lacked Hodgkin's intuition and imagination did not recognize the indications for pyrrole rings. She took over 2,500 X-ray photographs of vitamin B_{12} ($C_{63}H_{88}N_{14}O_{14}PCo$) over a six-year period. For analysis, Hodgkin sent her data by telegram and airmail to the University of California at Los Angeles, where the crystallographer Kenneth Trueblood and his colleagues ran it on a very sophisticated computer. The National Bureau of Standards Western Automatic Computer was on UCLA's campus, and they had programmed it to perform crystallographic calculations 100 times more rapidly than standard methods. Anxious to test their newly developed software, Trueblood had offered Hodgkin computational assistance at no cost. The structure of vitamin B_{12}, elucidated in the 1955 *Nature* article, "The Crystal Structure of the Hexacarboxylic Acid Derived from B_{12} and the Molecular Structure of the Vitamin," contained a structure new to organic chemists, a corrin ring, which is structurally similar to porphyrin.

In 1960, the Royal Society of London awarded Hodgkin the first Wolfson Research Professorship, a position she held until she retired from Oxford in 1976. For her determinations by X-ray techniques of the structures of important biochemical substances, Hodgkin received the Nobel Prize in chemistry for 1964, becoming the first British female recipient. In 1965, Queen Elizabeth awarded her Britain's Order of Merit, the highest honor any British citizen can receive.

Realization of the Potential

Internationally recognized, Hodgkin resumed doing what she loved—research. Long ago, even before she received her doctorate, the Nobel-winning chemist (1947) Sir Robert Robinson gave

Hodgkin a crystalline sample of insulin. A hormone important for maintaining proper levels of sugar in the blood, this particular protein consisted of 777 atoms, her most complex molecule yet. She filtered, grew, and regrew insulin crystals, collecting data from wet and dry samples. In 1939, she wrote a note to *Nature*, "X-Ray Measurements on Wet Insulin Crystals." Other molecular mysteries interrupted her 35-year-long research project on insulin, yet she always kept it in her thoughts.

She prepared derivatives from several different heavy atoms, a technically difficult task but one that paid off. Her lab group analyzed 70,000 X-ray spots and chugged through the onerous calculations. She graciously allowed one of her postdoctoral students, Thomas Blundell, to announce the results on the structure of insulin at an IUCr meeting at the State University of New York at Stony Brook in 1969. Two years later, Hodgkin's lab group refined their model to a resolution of 1.9 angstroms, but she still thought it needed improvement. In 1988, she published her last scientific paper, "The Structure of 2Zn Pig Insulin Crystals at 1.5 Angstroms Resolution," in the *Philosophical Transactions of the Royal Society of London*. Her research led to an understanding of insulin's behavior in solution, chemical reactivity, and folding properties. By expanding the capabilities of X-ray crystallography, she demonstrated to organic chemists the potential utility and superiority of the technique over the tedious tasks of chemical analyses and degradations.

Honored Mother of Crystallography

The Royal Society of London gave Hodgkin the Royal Medal in 1957 for her beautiful, complex analysis of vitamin B_{12}, as well as the Copley Medal in 1976. She became a foreign member of the Royal Netherlands Academy of Sciences (1956) and the American Academy of Arts and Sciences (1958). From 1976 to 1988, she served as president of the Pugwash Conferences on Science and World Affairs, whose purpose is to bring together scholars from around the globe in order to find ways to reduce the danger of armed conflict. She was elected chancellor of Bristol University in 1970 and worked much harder than the ceremonial title required

Medically Significant Choices

Dorothy Hodgkin was recognized among physical chemists for her amazing ability to see molecular structures in enigmatic diffraction patterns of spots on photographic plates. Her popular fame, however, lies in her intuitive choice of biomolecules to research. Not only were they chemically interesting, but they were also all medically important.

Cholesterol is a waxy substance produced in the liver of animals that lends structural rigidity to the cell membranes and acts as a biochemical precursor for manufacturing vitamin D and for the production of steroid hormones involved in the development and function of the reproductive system and in maintaining physiological homeostasis. The role of cholesterol in the development of heart disease has led to increased interest in this complex biomolecule.

The effectiveness of penicillin in treating bacterial infections that cause diseases such as pneumonia, syphilis, and gas gangrene in wounds led to a demand difficult to meet by early production meth-

for 18 years. Though she refrained from ever discussing politics in the laboratory in order to protect her students, her associations with communists caused conflicts as the Cold War worsened, and her beliefs prevented her from keeping too quiet. In the late 1980s, Hodgkin wrote one of her former research students, Margaret Thatcher, the only prime minister of Great Britain with a science degree, offering advice on how to improve relations with the Soviet Union. Though she had visited several times previously, Hodgkin was refused a visa to visit the United States for an important meeting on protein structure in 1953, and she had to fight to regain permission to visit. During her lifetime, she traveled to many different countries for the purpose of exchanging scientific knowledge and to improve relations.

ods. Pharmaceutical companies were very interested in knowing the structure of the drug naturally produced by the mold *Penicillium* in hopes of manufacturing it in bulk. Though solving the structure did not lead to its synthetic production, it did allow for the eventual manufacture of semisynthetic penicillins when bacteria developed resistance to natural penicillin.

Vitamin B_{12} is necessary for the manufacture of red blood cells that carry oxygen to the body's tissues through blood circulation. Pernicious anemia is a potentially fatal disease caused by the absence of a glycoprotein called intrinsic factor, which assists in the absorption of vitamin B_{12} in the intestines. The chronic disease can be successfully treated with intramuscular injections of vitamin B_{12}. Biochemists discovered a completely synthetic method for producing this vitamin in 1979.

Insulin is a protein hormone made by the pancreas that stimulates cells to absorb sugar from the bloodstream into the cell. Without insulin, the body's cells starve regardless of the amount of food ingested. Diabetics that are insulin deficient depend on administration of the hormone by shots or pumps. Recombinant DNA technology led to the production of human insulin in the laboratory, replacing its extraction from slaughtered cows or pigs.

Hodgkin's husband had passed away from emphysema in 1982. She suffered from rheumatoid arthritis for most of her life and officially retired in 1977, but it has been reported lightheartedly that she must not have realized that she was retired. In her later years, her debilitating disease in combination with a broken pelvis confined her to a wheelchair but did not prevent her from traveling internationally to scientific and peace conferences for years afterward; she attended the IUCr meeting in Beijing in 1993. She died at her home in Ilmington, at the age of 84, on July 29, 1994.

Hodgkin's colleagues and former students remember her extraordinary gentleness and natural authority, as well as her great memory and keen intuition. She had the ability to see molecules in

X-ray diffraction patterns and the confidence to tackle seemingly impossible challenges. Her solution of the molecular structures for cholesterol, penicillin, vitamin B_{12}, and insulin demonstrated that X-ray analysis was the best method for determining three-dimensional structures, especially when the classic approaches did not work. Today Hodgkin's achievements may seem trivial to students who have been trained in crystallography using very advanced, modern computers, but at the time she stood alone in her willingness to take risks for the advancement of X-ray crystallography.

CHRONOLOGY

1910	Dorothy Hodgkin is born in Cairo, Egypt, on May 12
1932	Earns a bachelor's degree from Oxford University and begins graduate studies at Cambridge University with J. D. Bernal
1934	Returns to Somerville College of Oxford University as a tutor and research fellow in chemistry
1937	Earns a doctorate degree from Cambridge University
1942	Begins studying penicillin
1945	Solves the structure of penicillin
1946	Becomes lecturer and demonstrator in chemistry at Oxford University and helps form the International Union of Crystallography
1948	Begins researching vitamin B_{12}
1956	Determines the structure of vitamin B_{12} and becomes a university reader in X-ray crystallography at Oxford University
1960	Becomes the first Wolfson Research Professor at Oxford University
1964	Wins the Nobel Prize in chemistry for her determinations by X-ray techniques of the structures of important biochemical substances

1965	Named to the Order of Merit
1969	Determines the structure of insulin
1971–88	Serves as chancellor of Bristol University
1977	Officially retires from Wolfson professorship
1994	Dies at her home in Ilmington, Warwickshire, England, on July 29

FURTHER READING

Biographical Memoirs of Fellows of the Royal Society of London. Vol. 48. London: The Royal Society, 2002. Full memoir of Hodgkin, written by a distinguished colleague for the premier scientific organization of Britain.

Ferry, Georgina. *Dorothy Hodgkin: A Life.* Cold Spring Harbor, N.Y.: Cold Spring Harbor Laboratory Press, 2000. Full-length biography of one of the century's greatest crystallographers.

McGrayne, Sharon Bertsch. *Nobel Prize Women in Science.* Washington, D.C.: Joseph Henry Press, 1998. Examines the lives and achievements of 15 women who either won a Nobel Prize or played a crucial role in a Nobel Prize–winning project.

Nobelprize.org. "The Nobel Prize in Chemistry 1964." Available online. URL: http://nobelprize.org/chemistry/laureates/1964/. Last modified June 16, 2000. Includes links to Hodgkin's biography, Nobel lecture, and other resources.

Olson, Richard, ed. *Biographical Encyclopedia of Scientists.* Vol. 3. New York: Marshall Cavendish, 1998. Clear, concise summary of major events in scientists' lives at an accessible level.

GLOSSARY

adsorption the process in which molecules come into contact with and adhere to a surface without being absorbed

alkaloid organic bases that contain carbon, hydrogen, nitrogen, and oxygen

alpha-helix a common structural motif of proteins in which a linear sequence of amino acids forms a spiral stabilized by hydrogen bonding

amino acid one of 20 naturally occurring organic molecules that are the building blocks of proteins

analytical chemistry the branch of chemistry concerned with analyzing the composition and quantities of elements or compounds in substances

anion a negatively charged atom or group of atoms

antibody a protein manufactured by the immune system that specifically recognizes and binds foreign substances in order to destroy or weaken them

antigen a molecule that elicits an immune response

ascorbic acid vitamin C

atom the smallest particle of an element that retains the composition of the element, consisting of protons and neutrons in a central nucleus surrounded by electrons

atomic mass the average mass of all *isotopes* of a given element, relative to the carbon-12 isotope

atomic number the number of protons in the nucleus of an atom

Avogadro's number the number of atoms or molecules in a mole of a substance; 6.023×10^{23}

benzene   a cyclic compound with the molecular formula C_6H_6

beta-pleated sheet   a common folding pattern of proteins in which the formation of hydrogen bonds between neighboring regions of a polypeptide creates a flattened, rigid structure

biochemistry   the branch of chemistry dealing with the chemical processes that occur in living organisms

calorimeter   a device that measures heat given off by or present in a body

calx (pl. calces)   a combination of a metal and oxygen; what remains after a metal has been burned

carbohydrate   sugars, starches, and related compounds made up of carbon, hydrogen, and oxygen

carbon   a nonmetallic chemical element with the atomic number six. With a valence of four, carbon atoms have unique binding properties and form the basis of the major groups of biological molecules

carbon dioxide   a compound of carbon and oxygen with the molecular formula CO_2

cation   a positively charged atom or group of atoms

chemical reaction   a process in which two or more substances combine and change each other

chemistry   the science that deals with the composition, structure, and properties of substances and the changes they undergo

cholesterol   a lipid molecule with a four-ringed steroid structure and the molecular formula $C_{27}H_{46}O$; important biologically as a component of cell membranes and as a precursor for synthesizing other steroid molecules

combustion   the process of burning, in which a nonmetal combines with oxygen gas

complement   a component of the immune system found in the blood that combines with antibodies to destroy bacteria and other foreign substances

compound   a chemical combination of two or more elements

cortisone   a steroid hormone made in the adrenal cortex that is used in treating arthritis and other ailments characterized by inflammation

covalent bond   a bond formed when two atoms each donate one valence electron to form an electron pair that is shared between the two atoms

critical temperature   the temperature of a substance above which it cannot be liquefied by pressure alone

crystal   a solid particle formed by the arrangement of atoms, ions, or molecules into a regular, repeating, characteristic pattern

dipole moment   a characteristic possessed by a molecule when the centers of negative and positive electric charge are separated

disaccharide   a carbohydrate consisting of two simple sugars, or monosaccharides. Lactose, maltose, and sucrose are all disaccharides

dissenter   a person who refuses to conform to the rules of a church

electron   a subatomic particle found outside the nucleus that contains a negative charge and is largely responsible for the bonding between atoms

electron affinity   the power of a free atom to draw electrons to itself

electronegativity   the power of an atom within a molecule to draw electrons to itself

electrophoresis   a technique used to separate particles based on differential movement resulting from an electric field

element   a pure substance that cannot be further broken down by chemical means; a basic building block of matter

enantiomers   a pair of molecules that are mirror images of one another

enzyme   a protein that catalyzes a specific chemical reaction

epimer   a compound that differs from its isomer in the relative positions of an attached hydrogen and hydroxyl group

epinephrine   a hormone secreted by the adrenal gland that acts to help the body deal with stressful situations; adrenalin

fixed air   term formerly used to describe carbon dioxide

fructose   a six-carbon simple sugar

glaucoma   a disease characterized by a pressure increase in the eyeball that results in retinal damage and loss of vision

glucose   a monosaccharide; the most common form of sugar found in the blood

glycerol   a thick, colorless liquid obtained from animal and vegetable oils and fats

glycogen   a polysaccharide made of glucose molecules used to store energy in animal cells

group   a vertical column in the periodic table. The elements in a group share similar chemical properties

gypsum   a mineral that is heated and then combined with water to make plaster

hemoglobin   the oxygen-carrying, iron-binding protein found in red blood cells

hormone   a chemical messenger made by one group of cells that travels through blood circulation to affect the activity of another group of cells

hybridization   in chemistry, the formation of hybrid atomic orbitals by various combinations of the s, p, and d ground-state atomic orbitals

hydrogen   the chemical element that has an atomic number of one

hydrogen bond   a weak chemical bond formed by the attraction of a slightly positive hydrogen atom with a partially negative atom of another molecule or region of the same molecule

hydrolysis   the breaking of a covalent bond by the addition of a water molecule. One product gains an –H atom and the other gains a –OH group

hydrophilic   polar, easily forms hydrogen bonds with water; it means "water-loving"

hydrophobic   nonpolar, does not dissolve in water; it means "water-hating"

inorganic chemistry   the branch of chemistry dealing with non-carbon-based compounds

insulin   a protein hormone necessary for the body to use sugar for energy and used to treat diabetes

ionic bond   an attractive force that holds together two ions with opposite electrical charges

isomers   different compounds that have the same molecular formula but different spatial arrangements of the atoms

isotopes   atoms with the same number of protons but different numbers of neutrons in the nucleus

Lewis dot structure   a method of notation in which the symbol of the element represents the nucleus and the core electrons. Dots placed around the symbol of the element represent the valence electrons

mannose   a six-carbon simple sugar

matter   in chemistry, any substance that has mass and occupies space

mercury   a metal that exists as a silvery liquid at room temperature

metabolism   the sum of all chemical reactions that occur in the cells of living organisms. Includes anabolic reactions that result in the biosynthesis of larger molecules from smaller molecules and catabolic reactions that break down complex molecules into simpler ones with an accompanying release of energy

molecular clock   a measurement of evolutionary time by the number of nucleotide substitutions

molecule   a combination of atoms joined together by covalent bonds

monosaccharide   a simple sugar such as glucose or fructose

neutron   a subatomic particle with no charge, found in the nucleus

nitrogen   an element with the atomic number seven. Nitrogen gas makes up 71 percent of the gas in the atmosphere

orbital   a subdivision of an energy level for an electron

organic chemistry   the chemistry of compounds with C–C and/or C–H bonds. Generally includes all the molecules that comprise living cells

oxygen   an element with an atomic number of eight that combines with other substances during combustion, or burning

penicillin   a chemical produced by the mold *Penicillium* that has powerful antibacterial properties

pepsin   a digestive enzyme secreted by the stomach that breaks down proteins

peptide bond   a chemical bond that links two amino acids

period   in chemistry, a horizontal row of the periodic table

periodic law   the recurrence of chemical properties of the elements when arranged by atomic number

periodic table a convenient means to present the chemical elements and information about them. The elements are arranged by atomic number with elements sharing similar chemical properties located in the same vertical group

phlogiston fire as a chemical substance, historically thought to be present in things that burn but does not really exist

phosphorylation the addition of a phosphate group. May change the activity of a molecule

photosynthesis the process by which some organisms use energy from sunlight to synthesize carbohydrates from carbon dioxide and water

physical chemistry the branch of chemistry that applies physical theories or laws to explain chemical behavior

physostigmine a medically useful alkaloid isolated from the Calabar bean; eserine

pneumatic chemistry the study of gases

pneumatic trough an apparatus used to collect gases

polypeptide a chain or polymer of amino acids

progesterone a steroid hormone important for the female reproductive system

protein a large, complex, biological molecule made up of amino acids. The major constituent of cells

proton a subatomic particle with a positive charge and found in the nucleus

purine a bicyclic, nitrogenous, ringed molecule, with the molecular formula $C_5N_4H_4$, that is a constituent of nucleic acids

resonance the fluctuation of molecules between two or more alternate structures, each containing the same atoms but with different electron arrangements

respiration a cellular process in which oxygen is consumed and carbon dioxide is produced, as in the breaking down of carbohydrates for energy

shell an energy level within an atom

steroid any of a large group of lipophilic molecules structurally related by a ringed structure, including cholesterol, certain vitamins, various hormones, and bile acids

sterol   a chemical belonging to a group of mostly unsaturated alcohols and found in plant and animal tissues

substrate   a substance that participates in a chemical reaction

sugar   a type of carbohydrate made of carbon, hydrogen, and oxygen with the general formula $(CH_2O)_n$

testosterone   a steroid hormone important for the development and function of the male reproductive system

thermochemistry   the study of heat associated with chemical reactions

valence   the number of electrons an atom must gain or lose in order to fill its outermost shell

valence shell   the outermost electron shell of a neutral atom

vitamin B_{12}   a vitamin that contains cobalt and is used to treat pernicious anemia

X-ray crystallography   a technique used by chemists in which X-rays are passed through a crystal and the diffraction pattern is interpreted to gain information about the three-dimensional atomic arrangement of molecules

FURTHER RESOURCES

Books

Brock, William H. *The Chemical Tree: A History of Chemistry.* New York: W. W. Norton and Company, 2000. Traces the roots of chemistry from the roots of alchemy through the 20th century.

The Diagram Group. *The Facts On File Chemistry Handbook.* New York: Facts On File, 2000. Convenient resource containing a glossary of terms, short biographical profiles of celebrated chemists, a chronology of events and discoveries, and useful charts, tables, and diagrams.

Greenburg, Arthur. *A Chemical History Tour: Picturing Chemistry from Alchemy to Modern Molecular Science.* New York: Wiley-Interscience, 2000. A tour of the discipline's history.

Hudson, John. *The History of Chemistry.* New York: Chapman and Hall, 1992. Describes the development of chemistry from the earliest times to the present. Includes biographical sketches of several pioneering chemists.

Knapp, Brian J. *Elements.* 18 vols. Danbury, Conn.: Grolier Educational, 2002. In-depth descriptions of the elements (through 118).

Lagowski, Joseph J., ed. *Macmillan Encyclopedia of Chemistry.* New York: Macmillan Reference USA, 1997. Explains the phenomena, concepts, and materials of chemistry and includes some biographical profiles.

———. *Chemistry: Foundations and Applications.* 4 vols. New York: Macmillan Reference USA, 2004. A comprehensive guide that explores the core concepts, history, and applications of chemistry.

Morris, Richard. *The Last Sorcerers: The Path from Alchemy to the Periodic Table*. Washington, D.C.: Joseph Henry Press, 2003. Depicts the careers of 18th-century scientists.

Oakes, Elizabeth H. *A to Z of Chemists*. New York: Facts On File, 2002. Profiles more than 150 chemists, discussing their research and contributions. Includes bibliography, cross-references, and chronology.

Reinhardt, Carsten, ed. *Chemical Sciences in the 20th Century: Bridging Boundaries*. New York: Wiley-VCH, 2001. Monograph of the revolutionary theories and experimental breakthroughs in chemistry as they relate to physics, biology, mathematics, and technology.

Rittner, Don, and Ronald A. Bailey. *Encyclopedia of Chemistry*. New York: Facts On File, 2005. Comprehensive reference of 800 A-to-Z entries encompassing definitions, issues, discoveries, biographies, and experiments.

Wertheim, Jane, Chris Oxlade, and Corrine Stockley. *The Usborne Illustrated Dictionary of Chemistry*. London: Usborne, 2000. Recommended for middle school students.

Internet Resources

BioChemHub. Available online. URL: http://biochemhub.com/biochem/biochemhub.cfm. Accessed February 6, 2005. Contains a listing of further resources for general chemistry categorized into high school chemistry, college chemistry, periodic tables, laboratory experiments, and inorganic molecules.

Chemistry Resources. EdInformatics.com, 1999. Available online. URL: http://www.edinformatics.com/chemistry.htm. Accessed February 6, 2005. Resources organized by subjects including analytical chemistry, atmospheric chemistry, elements, environmental chemistry, geochemistry, inorganic, organic chemistry, and many more.

Explore Chemical History. The Chemical Heritage Foundation, 2003. Available online. URL: http://www.chemheritage.org/explore/explore.html. Accessed February 6, 2005. Divided into sections titled "Matter and Molecules," "Innovation and

Industry," "Ancients and Alchemists," "Chemistry of Life," "Polymers: Molecular Giants," and "Chemical Information Science," with each containing time lines, short biographical profiles, and additional resources.

Giunta, Carmen. Classic Chemistry. Available online: URL: http:// web.lemoyne.edu/~giunta/. Accessed February 6, 2005. Contains daily tidbits about chemistry and numerous links to selected classic chemistry papers and calculations, a history of chemistry calendar, an online glossary, and other Internet resources related to the history of chemists, chemistry, and science.

Helmenstine, Anne Marie. "Chemistry." About, Inc., 2004. Available online: URL: http://chemistry.about.com. Accessed February 6, 2005. Read interesting features by following the "Articles and Resources" links. Visit the links found under "Essentials" to find an online encyclopedia, chemical structures, and definitions of chemical terminology.

Martindale, Jim. Martindale's The "Virtual" ~ Chemistry Center, 2004. Available online. URL: http://www.martindalecenter.com/ GradChemistry.html. Accessed February 6, 2005. Extremely resourceful site with numerous links to everything from chemistry journals, chemistry content review, tutorials, periodic tables, and databases.

The Nobel e-Museum: Chemistry. The Nobel Foundation, 2004. Available online. URL: http://nobelprize.org/chemistry/ educational/index.html. Last modified December 6, 2004. Contains links to different educational games for topics including polymers, chirality, PCR, biochemistry, and molecular biology.

Periodic Table. American Chemical Society, 2004. Available online. URL: http://www.chemistry.org/portal/a/c/s/1/home.html. Accessed February 6, 2005. Use scroll-down quick-find menu on left to access periodic table, then click on each element to reveal general information about that element and its electronic configuration.

The Science House: Countertop Chemistry. North Carolina State University. Available online. URL: http://www2.ncsu.edu/ncsu/ pams/science_house/learn/CountertopChem/index.html. Accessed February 6, 2005. Contains background science information and directions for performing chemistry demonstrations using ordinary household materials.

Senese, Fred. General Chemistry Online! Available online. URL: http://antoine.frostburg.edu/chem/senese/101/index.shtml. Last modified January 19, 2005. This Web site is a great starting place for Web searches. Be sure to visit the "FAQs," "Features," and "Just Ask Antoine!" links.

World of Molecules. Available online. URL: http://www.worldof molecules.com. Accessed February 6, 2005. A molecular database with text to supplement the structural images, organized into categories including food molecules, solvent molecules, fuel molecules, and more.

Periodicals

American Scientist

Published by Sigma Xi, The Scientific Research Society
P.O. Box 13975
3106 East NC Highway 54
Research Triangle Park, NC 27709
Telephone: (919) 549-0097 or (800) 282-0444
www.amsci.org/amsci/amsci.html
Bimonthly magazine containing articles on science and technology

ChemMatters

Published by the American Chemical Society
1155 Sixteenth Street, NW
Washington, DC 20036-4800
Telephone: (800) 227-5558
chemistry.org/education/chemmatters.html
Quarterly magazine for high school chemistry students

Discover

Published by Buena Vista Magazines
114 Fifth Avenue
New York, NY 10011

Telephone: (212) 633-4400
www.discover.com
A popular monthly magazine containing easy to understand articles
on a variety of scientific topics

Nature

The Macmillan Building
4 Crinan Street
London N1 9XW
Telephone: +44 (0) 20 7833 4000
www.nature.com/nature
A prestigious primary source of scientific literature

Science

Published by the American Association for the Advancement of
   Science
1200 New York Avenue, NW
Washington, DC 20005
Telephone: (202) 326-6417
www.sciencemag.org
One of the most highly regarded primary sources of scientific
research

Scientific American

415 Madison Avenue
New York, NY 10017
Telephone: (212) 754-0550
www.sciam.com
A popular monthly magazine that publishes articles on a broad
range of subjects and current issues in science and technology

Societies and Organizations

Alpha Chi Sigma Professional Chemistry Fraternity (http://www.
   alphachisigma.org) 2141 North Franklin Road, Indianapolis, IN
   46219. Telephone: (800) 252-4369

American Chemical Society (www.acs.org) 1155 Sixteenth Street, NW, Washington DC 20036. Telephone: 800-227-5558, 202-872-4600 (outside the U.S.)

Chemical Heritage Foundation (http://www.chemheritage.org) 315 Chestnut Street, Philadelphia, PA 19106. Telephone: (215) 925-2222

International Union of Pure and Applied Chemistry (http://www.iupac.org/dhtml_home.html) P.O. Box 13757, Research Triangle Park, NC 27709-3757. Telephone: (919) 485-8706

Royal Society of Chemistry (http://www.rcs.org) Burlington House, Piccadilly, London W1J 0BA. Telephone: +44 (0) 20 7437 8656

PERIODIC TABLE OF THE ELEMENTS

Key:
- Atomic number — 3
- Symbol — Li
- Atomic weight — 6.941

1 IA	2 IIA	3 IIIB	4 IVB	5 VB	6 VIB	7 VIIB	8 VIIIB	9 VIIIB	10 VIIIB	11 IB	12 IIB	13 IIIA	14 IVA	15 VA	16 VIA	17 VIIA	18 VIIIA
1 H 1.00794																	2 He 4.0026
3 Li 6.941	4 Be 9.0122											5 B 10.81	6 C 12.011	7 N 14.0067	8 O 15.9994	9 F 18.9984	10 Ne 20.1798
11 Na 22.9898	12 Mg 24.3051											13 Al 26.9815	14 Si 28.0855	15 P 30.9738	16 S 32.067	17 Cl 35.4528	18 Ar 39.948
19 K 39.0938	20 Ca 40.078	21 Sc 44.9559	22 Ti 47.867	23 V 50.9415	24 Cr 51.9962	25 Mn 54.938	26 Fe 55.845	27 Co 58.9332	28 Ni 58.6934	29 Cu 63.546	30 Zn 65.409	31 Ga 69.723	32 Ge 72.61	33 As 74.9216	34 Se 78.96	35 Br 79.904	36 Kr 83.798
37 Rb 85.4678	38 Sr 87.62	39 Y 88.906	40 Zr 91.224	41 Nb 92.9064	42 Mo 95.94	43 Tc (98)	44 Ru 101.07	45 Rh 102.9055	46 Pd 106.42	47 Ag 107.8682	48 Cd 112.412	49 In 114.818	50 Sn 118.711	51 Sb 121.760	52 Te 127.60	53 I 126.9045	54 Xe 131.29
55 Cs 132.9054	56 Ba 137.328	57-70 ☆	71 Lu 174.967	72 Hf 178.49	73 Ta 180.948	74 W 183.84	75 Re 186.207	76 Os 190.23	77 Ir 192.217	78 Pt 195.08	79 Au 196.9655	80 Hg 200.59	81 Tl 204.3833	82 Pb 207.2	83 Bi 208.9804	84 Po (209)	85 At (210)	86 Rn (222)
87 Fr (223)	88 Ra (226)	89-102 ★	103 Lr (260)	104 Rf (261)	105 Db (262)	106 Sg (266)	107 Bh (262)	108 Hs (263)	109 Mt (268)	110 Ds (271)	111 Rg (272)	112 Uub (277)	113 Uut (284)	114 Uuq (285)	115 Uup (288)	116 Uuh (292)	117 Uus ?	118 Uuo ?

☆ Lanthanoids

57 La 138.9055	58 Ce 140.115	59 Pr 140.908	60 Nd 144.24	61 Pm (145)	62 Sm 150.36	63 Eu 151.966	64 Gd 157.25	65 Tb 158.9253	66 Dy 162.500	67 Ho 164.9303	68 Er 167.26	69 Tm 168.9342	70 Yb 173.04

★ Actinoids

89 Ac (227)	90 Th 232.0381	91 Pa 231.036	92 U 238.0289	93 Np (237)	94 Pu (244)	95 Am 243	96 Cm (247)	97 Bk (247)	98 Cf (251)	99 Es (252)	100 Fm (257)	101 Md (258)	102 No (259)

Numbers in parentheses are atomic mass numbers of most stable isotopes

THE CHEMICAL ELEMENTS

(g) none (c) nonmetallics

element	symbol	a.n.
carbon	C	6
hydrogen	H	1

(g) chalcogen (c) nonmetallics

element	symbol	a.n.
oxygen	O	8
polonium	Po	84
selenium	Se	34
sulfur	S	16
tellurium	Te	52
ununhexium	Uuh	116

(g) alkali metal (c) metallics

element	symbol	a.n.
cesium	Cs	55
francium	Fr	87
lithium	Li	3
potassium	K	19
rubidium	Rb	37
sodium	Na	11

(g) alkaline earth metal (c) metallics

element	symbol	a.n.
barium	Ba	56
beryllium	Be	4
calcium	Ca	20
magnesium	Mg	12
radium	Ra	88
strontium	Sr	38

(g) none (c) metallics

element	symbol	a.n.
aluminum	Al	13
bohrium	Bh	107
cadmium	Cd	48
chromium	Cr	24
cobalt	Co	27
copper	Cu***	29
darmstadium	Ds	110
dubnium	Db	105
gallium	Ga	31
gold	Au***	79
hafnium	Hf	72
hassium	Hs	108
indium	In	49
iridium	Ir ****	77
iron	Fe	26
lawrencium	Lr	103
lead	Pb	82
lutetium	Lu	71
manganese	Mn	25
meitnerium	Mt	109
mercury	Hg	80
molybdenum	Mo	42
nickel	Ni	28
niobium	Nb	41
osmium	Os****	76
palladium	Pd****	46
platinum	Pt****	78
rhenium	Re	75
rodium	Rh****	45
roentgenium	Rg	111
ruthenium	Ru****	44
rutherfordium	Rf	104
scandium	Sc	21
seaborgium	Sg	106
silver	Ag***	47
tantalum	Ta	73
technetium	Tc	43
thallium	Tl	81
titanium	Ti	22
tin	Sn	50
tungsten	W	74
ununbium	Uub	112
ununtrium	Uut	113
ununquadium	Uuq	114
vanadium	V	23
yttrium	Y	39
zinc	Zn	30
zirconium	Zr	40

(g) prictogen (c) metallics

element	symbol	a.n.
arsenic	As*	33
antimony	Sb*	51
bismuth	Bi	83
nitrogen	N	7
phosophorus	P**	15
ununpentium	Uup	115

(g) none (c) semimetallics

element	symbol	a.n.
boron	B	5
germanium	Ge	32
silicon	Si	14

(g) actinoid (c) metallics

element	symbol	a.n.
actinium	Ac	89
americium	Am	95
berkelium	Bk	97
californium	Cf	98
curium	Cm	96
einsteinium	Es	99
fermium	Fm	100
mendelevium	Md	101
neptunium	Np	93
nobelium	No	102
plutonium	Pu	94
protactinium	Pa	91
thorium	Th	90
uranium	U	92

(g) halogens (c) nonmetallics

element	symbol	a.n.
astatine	At*	85
bromine	Br	35
chlorine	Cl	17
fluorine	F	9
iodine	I	53
ununseptium	Uus*	117

a.n. = atomic number
(g) = group
(c) = classification

(g) lanthanoid (c) metallics

element	symbol	a.n.
cerium	Ce	58
dysprosium	Dy	66
erbium	Er	68
europium	Eu	63
gadolinium	Gd	64
holmium	Ho	67
lanthanum	La	57
neodymium	Nd	60
praseodymium	Pr	59
promethium	Pm	61
samarium	Sm	62
terbium	Tb	65
thulium	Tm	69
ytterbium	Yb	70

(g) noble gases (c) nonmetallics

element	symbol	a.n.
argon	Ar	18
helium	He	2
krypton	Kr	36
neon	Ne	10
radon	Rn	86
xenon	Xe	54
unococtium	Uuo	118

* = semimetallics (c)
** = nonmetallics (c)
*** = coinage metal (g)
**** = precious metal (g)

Index